THE RINGS OF THE UNIVERSE

UBALDO de ROBERTIS

UBALDO de ROBERTIS

The Rings
of the Universe

Selected Poems

Translated by Adria Bernardi

To Rebecca
With all my best wishes—
gratitude— love—
the journey continues
amazing! thank you
un abbraccio—
Adria
January 17, 2017

 Chelsea Editions

Chelsea Editions, a press of Chelsea Associates, Inc., a not-for-profit corporation under section 501 (c) (3) of the United States Internal Revenue Code, has the support of the Sonia Raiziss Giop Charitable Foundation.

Cover art: Acruto Vitali (1903–1990), *Tastiere (Linguaggio dell'Universo)* / Keyboards (The Language of the Universe), 1963. Oil on canvas, 55 x 65 cm. Used by permission. Private collection.

Library of Congress Cataloging-in-Publication Data

Ubaldo de Robertis, 1942–
The Rings of the Universe: Selected Poems
Ubaldo de Robertis, translated by Adria Bernardi
p. 200

ISBN 978-0-9861061-5-6
1. de Robertis, Ubaldo—Translation into English
2. Bernardi, Adria, 1957–   II. Title

Manufactured in the United States of America by Thomson-Shore, Inc.

First Edition 2016

Chelsea Editions
Box 125, Cooper Station
New York, NY 10276-0125

www.chelseaeditionsbooks.org

CONTENTS

Translator's Note

. . . Thought penetrates into the stellar Universe to read
the animation iniside it that escapes us, in order to share in the
    irrepressible pulsar.

. . . Il pensiero si addentra nell'Universo stellare per leggervi
l'animazione che ci sfugge, per condividerne l'irrefrenabile pulsare.

from "The Universe and the Rings" (L'Universo e gli anelli)

"Kraik," the first poem of *Gli anelli dell'universo* (The Rings of the Universe)
begins with a sound from a contorted bird-like throat, *kraik* being an
onomatopoeic word that suggests a crackling and hissing bird call made in
irregular intervals. With this gesture, and this sound, the speaker posits and
then tests what will be the first of a multitude of questions: "And if these
shrill bent-neck heron cries were mine" (E se fossero mie queste stridule grida
d'airone dal collo piegato). The poet wants to explore "every new leaf," but he
is sometimes tormented by his own questions:

I think   sometimes   that life can be happy
without understanding
or feeling flattened by new ideas
so my face is never in contortions   and I'm never terrified
or afraid they might do
more harm.

Here, the poet, a researcher in nuclear chemistry, considers poetry as some-
thing that goes beyond the content of the experience, and the observation,
and connects the thought that emerges from the various fields of culture with
feeling, fantasy and imagination—as metaphysical world view in connection
with science tending toward something unitary. A link between existence,
values and meanings. What de Robertis calls "the report of its presence in
relation to the sense of life."

    Like "Kraik," the twelve poems of the first collection, *Diomedee* (Diomedes
2008) belong to the sounds—silence being one of them—of a landscape dense
with what is corporeal and material, birds, the desert, flowers, images that

accumulate even as a sense of physical weight, darkness, deep fatigue, and intense light builds. In "When Insomnia" (Quando l'insonnia), it is sleep distruption which is examined:

> When insomnia, infinite, endless
> leaves you thinking you're false, and contemptible,
> and vices run wild, and the liar's only interest is
> the dark passions of a world seducer and perverse, thoughts corrupt,
>
> (Quando l'insonnia sterminata infinita
> ti lascia credere falso, e vile
> e i vizi si scatenano, e il bugiardo sentire piega
> alle passioni ignote del mondo seduttore e perverso,)

But the moment of sleep noise, the momentary inability to sleep, even in its psychological impact, the poet says, doesn't lead to loss of interest or memory; rather to open the eyes *is* the conscience—the effort to keep up with the time he spends outside himself:

> When the extreme states of the soul, unwittingly,
> look for the place where solitude is most bitter, then, only then,
> does the spirit revolt pry off the crosses and the prison,
> privilege vindicates existing, the right demands
> surviving, the void breaks the piercing silence
> to listen to sounds, quivers,   harmonies.
>
> (Quando gli estremi stati d'animo cercano, inconsapevoli,
> il luogo dove più aspra è la solitudine, allora, soltanto allora,
> si ribella lo spirito, schioda le croci e la prigione,
> il privilegio rivendica di esistere, il diritto pretende
> di sopravvivere, il vuoto rompe lo straziante silenzio
> per ascoltare suoni, fremiti,   armonie.)

And always present in the poem we find sound, vibrations, movements, and the certainty is that energy is the matrix of the universe. That everything is wave, fluctuation and harmony. This theme, or perhaps better, this investigation and the methods of investigation from which it advances, cannot be made without sound, quivering—or vibration—and harmony, and it is this consideration of sound, of vibration and of harmony together, that constitutes one of the supporting structures that echo in the poems gathered from five collections and from de Robertis' unpublished poems as wave, interweaving, toward, backward, and forward again, arriving, at the volume's end in "Nella terra e nella musica" (In earth and music) and the title poem, "L'Universo e gli anelli" (The Universe and the Rings). There are verses of the poems that seem to emerge from the study of Physics and Cosmology, where the event makes the poem, revealing a poetics that is based on de Robertis' understanding of the structure of the world generated by quantic events where there are quantum fields delineating spacetime material and light, and where all space surrounding us is interwoven with quantum grains that vibrate between one event and another. A poem in which the poet asks, Where are these quantum of space? They are not in a space. They, themselves, are space. Science, the poem suggests, is like a continual exploration in ways of thinking. Throughout history, a great education was given by those who strove to improve the level of insight. One such extraordinary human is Newton:

> Newton climbed onto the shoulders of giants with his progression of
> colors
> and light for seeing farther, relating the world, where particles emerge
> from nothing, and fade away, out of reach, with their strangeness,
> even as rays of stars lost within their motion.

> (Sulle spalle dei giganti è salito Newton con il suo corteo di colori
> e di luce per vedere più avanti, e raccontare il mondo, dove dal nulla
> affiorano particelle, scompaiono con le loro stranezze, irraggiungibili,
> nemmeno fossero raggi di astri sperduti nel loro moto.)

Pythagoras, playing with numbers led to the discovery of the rule that the length of a cord and its corresponding vibrations produced intriguing sounds. Dante heard these sounds in his vision of Paradise in which all the orbits of the planets are in harmony: "Dante, il divino, sicuramente ha percepito il suono delle sfere, / riconosciuto come atto della mente: *l'armonia che temperi e discerni*." (Dante, the divine, surely had perceived the sound of the spheres, / recognized as an act of the mind: *l'armonia che temperi e discerni*)." This poem, in addition to serving as the title poem of the collection, also amplifies the meanings of the collection, and is intended to extend a universal vision, with the scientific cosmos and the most profound of visions being considered together in the same poem. It is a universe that maintains within itself the mystery of its existence. The poetry of de Robertis intends neither to disclose nor to unveil but rather to reveal some of its mecchanisms, including those that science has taught him: "And every unsettling concept about the Universe always surprises us. / What is it that's guiding reality? Ask! Questions mysteriously / live with us. Ask! Ask always, and again." (E sempre ci sorprende ogni concezione inquietante dell'Universo. / Ma che cosa guida la realtà? Domandare! Le domande ci abitano / misteriosamente. Domandare! Domandare sempre, e di nuovo.) The masters are recalled: Pythagoras, Dante, Newton—and for color, Kandinsky. It is thanks to these giants, scientists, thinkers, poets, artists, the poet can orient himself toward this higher level of insight in poems that carry on a dialogue of poetic inquiry about motion, light, matter, void, as in the poem, "Distant Stars" (Stelle lontane):

> On the stage
> of spacetime
> it all curves
> in arc dimensions
> under gravity's control
> which not even light
> can escape

But pay attention! the poem says. The purpose of knowledge is not only to reassure, cheer up; often knowledge disquiets and tears us up inside. As others have done in the past, de Robertis establishes a dialogue and raises questions through poetry on movement, light, matter, emptiness (which is never that) the stars, the motion of bodies, spatial relations, and reports the thought over time in his poetics, moving across landscapes, across deserts, in a tiring descent into hell, and a climb to the stars in search of truth as in a great lyrical symphony.

"Pyramids" (Piramidi) tells of moving across a desert and climbing toward the stars: "Parched earth, footprints on unmoving barren sands / on battered, deserted, unending routes." (Arsa la terra, impronte sulle sterili sabbie, inerti, / sulle rotte battute, deserti, sterminati.) The motives for climbing the pyramid of life are narrated: "I didn't climb up along the slope of pyramids / to the final peaks with crystal wings / and hands with a hundred fingers." (In alto non sono salito con ali di cristallo / e mani dalle cento dita lungo la china delle piramidi / fino alle strette vette.) And neither did he make the climb only to lose his way and flee but simply to look at the Moon: "It's that ... I couldn't sleep and I wanted to relish / the silent love of the Moon." (E' che ... non avevo sonno e volevo gustare / l'amore silenzioso della Luna.)

The collection *Diomedee* was followed by *Sovra il Senso del Vuoto* (2009), which was awarded the primo Premio Orfici, given in honor of Dino Campana; this was followed by the publication of *Se La Luna fosse un Aquilone* (2012). The fourth collection, *Quaderni dell'Ussero* (2013), takes its name from Caffè dell'Ussero, a gathering place of intellectuals established in Pisa in 1794 during Italian Risorgimento, which included poet Giusuè Carducci among its members. L'Accademia Nazionale dell'Ussero di Arti, Lettere e Scienze has its origins in the Caffè dell'Ussero; Ubaldo de Robertis is a member of this academy.

Echoing poems from the earlier collections, the opening poem of *Parti del discourso (poetico)*, begins on a primordial earth, with a climb from a desert to a pinnacle and looking up toward something higher and more illuminated—the sky and thought. The first poem of this collection, "Acque sotto il cielo un solo luogo," (begins with the verb *osservare*, observation being a requisite of investigative thought, discovery, and imagination: "Osservare impacciati naviplani / risalire fondali per mostrare / il mondo qual era" (Observing ungainly flyingboats rising from seafloors to show / what the world was). Waters beneath sky are glimpsed, and the vector of a de Robertis poem is again vertical; by looking up and down one might see what is revealed in its parts: "Acque sotto il cielo / un solo luogo / suddiviso tra abisso e rive / di uno stesso perduto paradiso" (Waters beneath the heavens / one place alone / split between abyss and shores / of the same lost paradise). The reader is invited to return to origins and to consider a multiplicity of viewpoints in looking at subject and object within space.

In "Ritratto del Padre" (Portrait of the Father), one of the final poems of the collection, the viewer stands before *Albrecht Dürer the Elder*, by Albrecht Dürer in the Uffizi Gallery in Florence, depicting the father who wears a black garment under a violet tunic. In the poem, the viewer considers his own father's reserve: "nessuno slancio da parte sua a svelare l'anima" (not one impulse coming from him to reveal the soul). The son, who describes himself as a rebel, analyzes his own distance and his reserve: "contrapporsi scindersi tenersi fuori separati distinti" (counterposing differentiating keeping a distance separated distinct" and encounters his father again as child: "eppure era stato lui a guidarti / eppure era stato lui a guidarti" (it was him in fact guiding you / on the first steps of sounds).

The influence of the poets who have preceded resonates within the poetry of Ubaldo de Robertis, and this is evident in examining, for example, the poem, "Formiche" (Ants): "Nel breve periodo tutte erano in vita. / Non vive veramente. / Vive nell'indifferenza." (For a short time they were all living, /

Not really living. / Living in indifference.) With echoes of Leopardi and Montale, the rings of a de Robertis poem widen, taking into consideration Montale's "Meriggiare pallido e assorto" from *Ossi di Seppia*, in which the tireless movement of the ants on a wall is contemplated as a metaphor for the life unexamined and the movement toward death. The de Robertis poem then expands to take in Leopardian imagery, tones, and colorations, raising questions about darkness and light, depths of destruction, meditations upon mortality, and the question of indifference raised in "La Ginestra," a poem that begins with an image of a group of ants on a tree at the foot of Mt. Vesuvius. As in "La Ginestra," which refers to a "popol di formiche," "Formiche," the poem by de Robertis, suggests a community of ants, a community of nameless human beings: "It didn't occur to anyone to give names. / Each was unknown even to itself." (A nessuno veniva in mente di dar loro un nome. / Sconosciute anche a se stesse.) Two elements are worth noting, one being de Robertis' lexical choice of the verb *franare* (E non hanno fatto in tempo ad echeggiare, / prima di franare nell'oblio), and the description of a world fallen apart in landslide as the ants fall into the earth's chasms. In "La Ginestra," the phrase, "E infranse e ricoperse," is followed by a description of a plunge into cataclysmic destruction. In both poems, the ants toil away in obliviousness as the poem progresses toward the description of disaster that awaits them. In the Leopardi poem, nature is indifferent to humans, while in the de Robertis poem, indifference is ascribed to the ants and those who did not think to name them. And once again, de Robertis raises a question: what would it be like to live a life of indifference?

In the poem, "Grattacielo" (Skyscraper), de Robertis returns to consider verticality in the context of "Il Grattacielo," by philospher and social scientist Max Horkheimer: "This building, whose basement is a slaughterhouse and whose roof is a cathedral, whose upper floor windows assure a beautiful view of the starry heavens." (Questo edificio, la cui cantina è un mattatoio e il cui tetto è una cattedrale, dalle fenestre dei piani superiori assicura effettivamente una bella vista sul cielo stellato.) The de Robertis poem asks whether the structure should be viewed from below or from above, suggesting the vector moves in more than one direction:

> it's only you Heraclitus affirming:
> "the path up and down are one and the same"
> more coherent thinking there are
> two orientations
> of a single insensate direction

In "Galileo," a statement of gratitude is made to the Pisan scientist:

> You who put your life   to the test
> for one new star, determined to disperse,
>   and in presenting again, the proof of a changeable universe
> that reason shocks,   and the great design
> of which its part   appeared   I am grateful to you,

In "Ho quasi consumato" (I have almost consumed), spacetime and human existence are explored together, as the impossibility of escaping gravitational force is recalled: "you can only enter through that door / not even the light / . . . will get out . . . / time itself will slow / its course" (da quella porta si può solo entrare / neppure la luce /. . . uscirà /. . . il tempo stesso rallenterà / il suo corso). The poem explores the black hole, but representation is compared here to the personal context. The poem arrives, at a a spiral of light—finally!—even in the depths of a black hole—and the color green, with its suggestion of hope:

> some of those who spun
> near me
> near the blue sphere
> of my dreams
> it will escort what I have only imagined
> it will play host to my present
> my past
> inside its own sphere
> near its own green
> distant
> personal
> future
>
> (qualcuno di quelli che hanno ruotato
> accanto a me
> prossimi all'azzurra sfera
> dei miei sogni
> scorterà ciò che ho soltanto immaginato
> ospiterà il mio presente
> il mio passato
> dentro la propria sfera

verso il suo verde
lontano
personale
futuro)

Color, de Robertis reminds us, is simply the frequency, the speed of the oscil-
lation of electromagnetic waves that form light. We see color all around us.
Throughout the poetry of de Robertis, we see color and light, and perception
of light, often times through painters, such as Kandinsky and Courbet. If
the waves vibrate more slowly, light will be red; if they vibrate more rapidly,
light is blue. Between the object and viewer are vibrating waves that carry the
images of the object all the way to us.

The virtue of the poetry of Ubaldo de Robertis lies in the bringing
together of a coinciding of the equilibria of the cosmos and the poet's own
spirit. From this fusion and from the great syntony the two worlds the poem
in its entirety is born. In the universe of de Robertis, a mysterious concert of
sounds gathers, an impercepitible musicality, as in Baudelaire, connecting all
things together and which only the poet is able to hear with his sixth sense.

ADRIA BERNARDI

THE RINGS OF THE UNIVERSE
Selected Poems

da DIOMEDEE

from DIOMEDES

Kraik

E se fossero mie queste stridule grida d'airone dal collo piegato
se fossi io a spargere su ogni foglia   nuova
la schiumosa saliva delle serpi   la prova
che striscio ogni volta l'istinto arrogante la ragione insidia
e pensieri ordinari (da non raccontare neanche a se stessi)
premono senza capire per cosa si vive
Mi chiedo   alle volte   specialmente di notte
quando non sono disposto a soffrire
come alla luce del giorno
quando esala l'orina dei gatti intorno
alle mie parole scagliate ad occhi chiusi
fra intermittenti ventate di pollini
che non possono mutare il senso di tutto l'insieme
o richiamare profumi di terre lontane
perché il presente mi giunga da tanto dolore
La mia storia   è soltanto sfiorare segrete ferite
con gesti che bruciano come raggi cocenti di sole
non onde leggere o echi di voci gradite.
Penso   alle volte   che possa essere lieta
la vita pur senza capire
o sentirsi schiacciare da idee nuove
per non storcere il viso   per non spaventarsi
o temere che possano fare
ancora più male.

Kraik

And if these shrill bent-neck heron cries were mine
if only it were me who spread out over every new   leaf
foamy snake saliva   the ordeal
I drag myself through every time instinct arrogant reason and
    ordinary
thoughts snaring (not to be told even to themselves)
they crush without understanding the purpose of living
I ask myself   at times   especially at night
when I'm not inclined to suffer
as in full daylight
when the urine from cats is exhaled all around
my words pounced with closed eyes
between intermittent pollen gusts
and it still wouldn't change the sense of all of it
or bring back fragrances of faraway lands
because the present links me with so much pain
My story   is only licking secrets wounds
with gestures that burn like the sun's scorching rays
not soft waves or echoes of pleasant voices.
I think   sometimes   that life can be happy
without understanding
or feeling flattened by new ideas
so my face is never in contortions   and I'm never terrified
or afraid they might do
more harm.

Quando ero

Quando ero un'altra cosa
un putto di una fontana o d'una chiesa
il mio aspetto poco contava

Stille di idee e sentimenti
fugavano da sole le tenebre
senza bisogno di talismani o rosari

Ora che l'inflessibile tempo
indifferente alla mia storia
spianta le radici e le prosciuga
le labbra mordo perché quelle stille
non acquistino voce

When I was

When I was something else
a *putto* in a fountain or in a church
my appearance didn't much matter

Drops of ideas and emotions
no need for rosaries or talismen
the darkness fled alone

Indifferent to my story
inflexible time now
pulls up roots and dries them
I bite my tongue so those silences
won't find their voice.

Come si può

Come si può mostrare una storia
se la memoria soggiace e dileguano immagini
fra le rughe del tempo.
E poi non soffia più lo stesso vento,
solo polvere sulle coppe argentate,
gli errori ammessi, le malinconie.
I desideri cadono come tenere gocce di pioggia
che nessuno raccoglie,
e al ruscello vanno bisbiglianti, impaurite.
Come si fa a narrare una storia,
una storia di bruma
se io non so   cosa sono stato.

How do you?

How do you tell a story
if memory underlies   and images vanish
among the creases of time?
And then if the same wind isn't blowing anymore,
only dust on silver-plated trophies,
admitted errors, sadnesses.
Desires fall like gentle raindrops
no one collects,
going into the stream fearful and whispering.
How it's possible to narrate a story,
a hazy story
if I don't know   what I was.

Altre sere

Altre sere sono io
quel lampadario che pende dal soffitto
che appena si accende brucia la pelle
meglio arrostire d'un colpo che ogni giorno un poco
e non sentire il peso di questo mio fardello
solo che al posto dei quanti e della luce
è un truce gioco di sangue che inonda la gola
solo che le vene sono asciutte e intorno alla lingua
  denti di cartone
Altre sere sono io a stendermi per terra
ad esibirmi in cadenze di danza
a suonare sulle cedevoli natiche fantasie variazioni
e mi riuscirebbero più graditi falsi accordi
o miserandi grugniti
Altre sere sono io a schiudere le labbra
adducendo sermoni ma è come masticare ghianda
quale parte avrei di questo prossimo duro severo cospiratore
    inferocito
pronto a squarciare a strapparmi il cuore
che prima d'essere per due terzi maturo è già marcito
Questa inquietudine mi assale quando s'approssima la notte
al mattino arrossisco e   rinfodero il pugnale

Other evenings

Other evenings that's me
that chandelier hanging from the ceiling
the skin burning as soon as it's turned on
better to be grilled all at once than a little bit each day
and not feel the weight of the load I haul around
except in place of quantum and light
is cruel blood-game that floods the throat
except the veins are dried up and the teeth
  cardboard on the tongue
Other evenings that's me stretched out along the ground
showing off in dance cadences
playing fantasy variations on soft buttocks
and it would result in more accepted false musical chords
or pitiful grunts
Other evenings that's me lips parting
expounding sermons except it's like chewing an acorn
that part I'd have of this next hard severe enraged conspirator
ready to tear   to rip out my heart
already gone bad before it's even two-thirds ripe
This apprehension attacks me as night gets close
in the morning I blush and   I put the dagger back into its
    sheath

Quando l'insonnia

Quando l'insonnia sterminata infinita
ti lascia credere falso, e vile
e i vizi si scatenano, e il bugiardo sentire piega
alle passioni ignote del mondo seduttore e perverso,
i pensieri si corrompono, l'istinto si abbevera
di cattive apparenze, iene che vogliono uscire
all'aperto nel dominio di esseri invisibili.

Quando gli estremi stati d'animo cercano, inconsapevoli,
il luogo dove più aspra è la solitudine, allora, soltanto allora,
si ribella lo spirito, schioda le croci e la prigione,
il privilegio rivendica di esistere, il diritto pretende
di sopravvivere, il vuoto rompe lo straziante silenzio
per ascoltare suoni, fremiti,   armonie.

Fiera e dolce come un gatto nottambulo
la mente spazia oltre il limite,
l'anima si disseta di stelle, di parole dense, immagini nuove.
Ecco! si scrive soltanto per uscire   dall'inferno.

When Insomnia

When insomnia, infinite, endless
leaves you thinking you're false, and contemptible,
and vices run wild, and the liar's only interest is
the dark passions of a world seducer and perverse,
thoughts corrupt, instinct waters brutal appearances,
hyenas that want to go out
into the open into the domain of invisible creatures.

When the extreme states of the soul, unwittingly,
look for the place where solitude is most bitter, then, only then,
does the spirit revolt, pry off the crosses and the prison,
privilege vindicates existing, the right demands
surviving, the void breaks the piercing silence
to listen to sounds, quivers,   harmonies.

As ruthless and gentle as a cat walking around
at night the mind ranges beyond the limits,
the soul waters itself with stars, with crowding words, new
        images.
This is Why! You write just to get out of   hell.

La Sfida

Afferrare
un ramo con destrezza
ferendoci all'improvviso

Rivoli dal profondo
come vermiglia linfa
a coprire la pelle
Gemme che la mano rovescia
e un calice raccoglie
immaginario

Pensare
come vorrebbe
la foglia gialla
immersa in tanta luce
quel colore
per reggere   la sfida
con la rosa

The Challenge

To grab
a branch with skill
suddenly wounding ourselves

Trickles from deep
like vermillion sap
covering the skin
Buds the hand spills
and an imaginary goblet
collects

To think
it would take
the yellow leaf
submerged in that much light
that color
to endure   the challenge
with the rose.

Piramidi

Arsa la terra, impronte sulle sterili sabbie, inerti,
sulle rotte battute, deserti, sterminati.
Carovane, cammelli accovacciati,
falde profonde, vento sui palmeti,
sui lembi delle tende aperte alle brezze,
aspidi sulle dune, sciami di locuste, agguati.
Io non ho calzato zoccoli di luce,
indossato piume, né gemme colorate
per sfidare gli occhi oscuri della notte.
In alto non sono salito con ali di cristallo
e mani dalle cento dita lungo la china delle piramidi
fino alle strette vette.
Non sono salito per scrutare orizzonti lontani,
azzurri, trasparenti, o cieli sempre più vicini.
Non sono salito per far perdere le mie tracce,
o per cercare la mia genia, per mettermi in salvo,
o per innalzare preghiere.
E'   che . . . non avevo sonno e volevo gustare
l'amore silenzioso della Luna.

Pyramids

Parched earth, footprints on unmoving barren sands
on battered, deserted, unending routes.
Caravans, camels hunkered down, deep
layers, wind on palm groves,
on the edges of tents open to breezes,
asps on dunes, swarms of locusts   snares.
I'm not wearing light-up clogs,
wings on shoulders, or colored gems
to challenge the night's dark eyes.
I didn't climb up along the slope of pyramids
to the final peaks with crystal wings
and hands with a hundred fingers.
I didn't climb up here to gaze at blue, transparent, far off
horizons, or at even closer skies.
I didn't climb in order to lose my way
or to seek out my own kind, to save myself,
or to rise up in prayer.
It's that . . . I couldn't sleep and I wanted to relish
the silent love of the Moon.

Sopra una visione di E. A. Poe

Non l'ho amata dunque? sicuro che l'ho amata,
da tanto, tanto tempo e . . .   l'amo ancora,
eppure, soltanto i miei occhi la seguirono,
oh! se fossi morto nell'istante
Lei non l'avrebbe saputo,
non osavo, non osavo parlare,
io, inerme, impietrito, trafitto,
non osavo /ti dico/ non osavo parlare.

Ora che la mia ispida barba
larghi chiarori improvvisa, l'irriducibile attesa
si fa più grande.

Il mio primo amore /ti dico/ è come la pioggia amica,
non si annuncia, la senti arrivare,
ascolta,   ora è qui, silenziosa,
ritta, sulla mia soglia
in attesa che io scrolli
la muffa grigia dalla mia porta.

On a Vision of E. A. Poe

So I didn't love her? I must have loved her,
for a long time, a very long time and . . . I still love her,
and yet, only my eyes accompanied her,
oh! if I had died in that moment
She would not have known it,
I did not dare, I did not dare to speak,
defenseless, petrified, stabbed, I
I did not dare /I tell you/ I did not dare to speak.

Now that my bristly beard
is improvising large glimmers, the unrelenting wait
grows even   larger.

My first love /I tell you/ is like friend rain,
it's not announced, you feel her arrive,
listen,   she's here now, silent,
standing, on my doorstop
waiting for me to shake off
the gray mold from my door.

La mia fatica

La mia fatica è . . .
reggere la testa tra le mani di ghiaccio
convincermi di un qualcosa che conti rispettare le regole
rammentare il numero dell'autobus
  /non ferma sempre allo stesso punto/
La mia paura è
l'inchiostro rosso che scolora, come i capelli,
come gocce d'urina sul carbone,
la pelle slavata /quando il sole imperversa a cuocere la terra/.
La mia fatica è . . .
togliere il sapone giallo dalla schiena /grassa e mal lavata/,
un frammento di carne tra i denti,
salire all'altezza delle lampade.
La mia paura è . . .
che non ritorni il libro /dal prestito/,
uscire dalla sala di lettura /senza ombrello/,
chiedere il conto, /rimpiangere il bordello/
sapere che tra milioni di bestie
l'unico ad avere un'anima è l'uomo
/ è migliore d'ogni altra specie?/
La mia fatica è . . .
ascoltare Mozart e non . . . soffrire,
la prova generale della commedia
l'inventare me stesso/ogni volta/,
accettare che tutto è annunciato /come l'ultimo canto del cigno/.
La mia paura è
incontrarmi seduto /su di un paracarro/e rabbrividire.
Prenderti tra le braccia
e cadere al suolo, a piombo, tramortito.

My exhaustion

My exhaustion is . . .
holding up my head between hands of ice
convincing myself of one thing that matters in following rules
remembering the number of the bus
   /it doesn't always stop at the same place/
My fear is
red ink that fades, like hair,
like drops of urine on coal,
washed-out skin /when the unrelenting sun is baking the earth/.
My exhaustion is . . .
getting the yellow soap off my back /fat and not well washed/,
a piece of meat between the teeth,
climbing up as high as the light fixtures.
My fear is . . .
that I won't return the book /on loan/,
leaving the reading room /without an umbrella/,
asking for the bill, /regretting the mess/
knowing that among millions of animals
the only one that has a soul is man
/ is he better than every other species?/
My exhaustion is . . .
listening to Mozart and not . . . suffering,
the final rehearsal of the comedy
the inventing of myself/each time/,
accepting that everything's announced./like the swan song/.
My fear is
meeting myself seated /on a road divider/and shivering.
Taking you in my arms
and falling to the ground, straight down, stone dead.

Rosa Gallica

Non tra
le siepi di ligustro
i fiori recisi dell'iris
i calici dell'ibisco dalle cinque punte
le invadenti stelle del gelsomino
o il solitario fiore del tulipano
Non fra
i mirabili cespugli della bella di notte
le cuoriformi foglie che propiziano amori
e gettano intriganti colori al tramonto
ma
dentro il cerchio di una rosa gallica
svettante sul ramo più bruno e spinoso
in un petalo nascosto vellutato
trovai scritto il tuo nome
ma
tu mi dicesti
che non era il tempo
di legare le rose

Rosa Gallica

Not among
the wax-leaf privets
the cut flowers of irises
the calyxes of the hibiscus with five points
the invasive stars of the jasmine
or the solitary flower of the tulip
Not among
the amazing shrubbery of night's beauty
the heart-shaped leaves that bring on love
and toss intriguing colors to the sunset
but
inside the circle of a Gallic rose
standing out on top of a browner and thorny stem
in a velvety hidden petal
I found your name written
but
you said to me
that it wasn't the time
to be tying up roses

Capelli aguzzini

Capelli aguzzini
groviglio di serpi
profumi di terre piovane,
di nuovo la tua mano . . .
asilo di accattoni.
Ti seguirò cigno incosciente
asina astuta.
Ti frusterò piede smarrito.
Ordinerò alle vene di cercarti
giunca veloce, talpa vagabonda.
Gli indovini mi diranno
dove la notte dormi
piccola balena danzante.
Per te mi addoloro volentieri,
Amore tormentato.

Tormentor's Hair

Tormentor's hair
knot of snakes
scents of rained-on earth,
your hand again . . .
refuge for rejects . . .
Unconscious swan
astute ass I'll follow you.
Misguided missteps I'll whip you.
Speedy junk boat, vagabond mole
I'll take full command looking for you.
You will guess it they will tell me
where you sleep at night
little dancing whale.
Excruciating Love,
I'm in pain for you willingly.

Sopra un adagio di J. Haydn

Per quanto tempo ancora dovrò fiutare il vento . . .
Ovunque scomposte grida, dissennate parole d'ordine.
La mancanza di voci sagge.
E' il senso di tetraggine che mi sconcerta,
nel mondo sovraccarico di esseri inquieti.

Quando mi passarono accanto, le straniate armature
di uomini irriducibili, obbligati a convincermi
sugli elementi morali della guerra,
nel loro volto metallico, nei loro occhi iniettati,
colsi in tutta la reale dimensione,
la misura del mio terrore e della mia sconfitta.
Presto dovrò coricarmi prima che faccia sera.

Over an adagio by J. Haydn

How much longer will I have to keep sensing what's in the
      wind . . .
Screaming insane rude rallying cries everywhere.
The lack of wise voices.
It's the sense of bleakness that disturbs me,
in the world overwhelmed with anxious creatures.

When they passed on my side, the alienated armor
of relentless men, obliged to convince me
of the moral factors of war,
in their metal faces, in their injected eyes,
captured the royal dimensions of it all,
the scope of my terror and my defeat.
I'll have to go to bed early before it gets dark.

da SOVRA IL SENSO DEL VUOTO

from ABOVE THE SENSE OF THE VOID

Il tempo

Il tempo,
occhi d'acciaio,
morde la pelle, preme
sulla venatura,
su tutti i rami delle ossa,
nulla che possa
del suo eterno movimento
umiliarmi,
se mi lamento è solo per
intenerirti.
Un piccolo cedimento
ad ogni giro di ruota,
la vita inutile vuota,
o è il vuoto della vita?
di qualsiasi vita.
La realtà, terribile, si svela.
Io . . . io l'ho immaginata
la notte. Temibile,
indistinta,
il lungo, il duro assedio,
arrendersi
al nulla che c'è intorno,
al gelo che rende il cuore
vuoto, da rendere,
da restituire al   vuoto.

Time

Time,
steel eyed,
eats away at the skin, presses
down on the veining,
on each ramus among the bones,
nothing that can
humiliate me
with its eternal movement,
if I complain it's only because
I want to move you.
A small concession
to every turn of the wheel,
life as useless void
or it void of life?
of any life whatever.
Reality, horrible, reveals itself.
I . . . I imagined it
night. Intimidating,
indistinct,
the long, the hard, siege
surrendering to
the nothing that's all around,
with the freeze that turns the heart into
void, to be turned into,
to be returned to the   void.

Ténéré

Onde lontane, ripercosse, passate sotto silenzio,
avvicendate da foreste infeconde,
forme ineffabili somiglianti al naufragio.

Qui non era . . . il deserto

Abbarbicati alle muraglie,
pensieri grigioterra, sabbia e cenere,
taluni umilianti,
tentano tutti insieme di scomporre
segmenti di solitudine,
desuete, estenuate parole,
per esortare la vita che sfiorisce.

Se era polvere . . . . l'Uomo
Cos'è dunque il . . . Sahara . . .

Ténéré

Distant waves, echoes, pasts beneath silence,
alternated by sterile forests,
indescribable forms resembling shipwreck.

It was not desert . . . here

Clinging to rock walls,
earthgray thoughts, sand and ash,
some humiliating,
all try together to break
segments of silence into pieces,
obsolete, worn out words,
to encourage life to blossom.

If Man was . . . . dust
What then is the . . . Sahara . . .

Commiato

Mettermi in viaggio
finché sarò vecchio /di affanni/
verso il confine
che lo sguardo prolunga
all'infinito,
per scovare sentieri,
virtuosi pensieri,
l'invito a ritrovare
me stesso.
Poi, . . . stanco,
il paltò consumato,
tornare sui gradini
della vecchia casa
e sedermi consolato.
Accogliere
l'indifferenza dei vicini
come fosse
un   nuovo   addio.

Farewell

Send me off travelling
until I'm old /with worries/
in the direction of the border
I extend to the infinite
with my eyes
for an extended period,
to uncover paths,
virtuous thoughts,
the invitation to find myself
again.
Then, . . . tired,
overcoat worn-out,
go back up the steps
of the old house
and sit down consoled.
Welcoming
the neighbors' indifference
as if it were
a   new   goodbye.

Le Rondini

Come fischiano le rondini intorno alla chiesa
—L. Sinisgalli

E' tutta in un volo di ali appuntite
la bella stagione
lucente nei crepuscoli
sfumati di ruggine
orlati da bande blu
controvento
festanti
La vita è vita
Vit vit
vit vit   trilli pungenti
Solo gemiti dai sottotetti
lacrime come acquesante quante
ne contengono nidi ripudiati
tiepidi bordi di paglia e fango
Cade lo sguardo alle grondaie tappate
Dal piedistallo dei ricordi . . .
rochi rimpianti

Swallows

The way swallows around the church screech
—L. Sinisgalli

It's all in a flight of those pointy wings
in the beautiful season
lit in twilights
tinged with rust
edges of blue layers
windward
joyous
Life is life
Vit vit
vit vit   piercing trills
Just moans from the attics
tears like holy water   so much of it
pooling inside abandoned nests
with damp edges of straw and mud
The gaze drops to the gutter blocked
by the memory pedestal . . .
hoarse   regrets

Sollers tempus

Nessun altro, indifferente,
all'infuori del sonno,
può sospendere l'effetto ruota
di pietra nera
che consegna la mente,
insinuata dall'assuefazione
al futuro.

Non ali di farfalla, fiori di lavanda,
ma lembi in rapida consunzione,
pelle dell'acre afrore di zolfo
che la cenere sommuove.

Il tempo   è così solerte con me,
ne ho le prove
e dovrei ancora riscattarmi,
ma non so quando
né dove
non so   come.

Sollers tempus

Nobody else, indifferent,
when not asleep,
can suspend the wheel
effect of the black stone
that turns in the mind
wheedled by the habit
of the future.

Not butterfly wings or flowers of lavender
but leaves in quick decay,
rinds of bitter sulfur stink
that ash agitates.

Time   is so diligent with me,
I have the evidence
and I'd still have to ransom myself
but don't know when
or where either
I do not know   how.

Da lontano, molto da lontano . . .

Da lontano, molto da lontano, immensamente verde
l'infanzia rovesciata sull'erba a rubare immagini
visto che nessuno si prende cura di te,
frutto che cade frettoloso prima d'essere colto.
Cortili bisacce unte arrotini affila coltelli temperini,
grembi di donne occhi marroni fazzoletti bianchi
impastate di terra da capo a piedi.
Panieri   brocche di terracotta vino asprigno che trabocca.
Quasi a sfiorare l'azzurro alberi altissimi,   ombre lunghe,
ombre molto più grandi di te, treni settecarrozze
attraversano la pianura, piccoli mondi di storie silenziose.
No. Non voglio che la clessidra si vuoti. Non voglio
rientrare in quei mondi, ma neppure che mi escano dalla mente.
Mi basta un solo attimo per ritornare, per restare in vettura.
All'inizio,   aria pura. Tutto era connesso e . . . verde.
Misteriosamente, immensamente verde.

From a distance, a great distance . . .

From a distance, a great distance, expansively green
childhood turned inside out in grass stealing images
given that you have no caretaker
unripened fruit falling scattershot.
Courtyards oily sacks knife grinders sharpening penknives
women's laps nut brown eyes white handkerchiefs
smeared head to foot with dirt.
Baskets   terracotta jugs sharp wine spilling over.
Trees so tall they graze the sky,   long shadows,
shadows so much larger than you are, trains made of only
seven carriages trains crossing the plain,
little worlds of silent stories.
No. I don't want the hourglass to be empty. I don't want
to go back into those worlds. But neither do they leave my mind.
It takes only a moment to go back there, to be back for the all
        aboard.
At the start, clean air. It was all connected and . . . green.
Mysteriously, expansively green.

da SE LA LUNA FOSSE UN AQUILONE

from IF THE MOON WERE A KITE

Presagio

Fuori del mare . . .
alberi svestiti di vele
la sferza dei venti che scompiglia
drizze di randa ed amantigli
schiume increspate
fremono   in muraglie

Sarà il nocchiere
creatura senza nome
uomo dello scandaglio
non l'opera morta
non l'immersa carena
ad aprirsi in squarci
a cedere . . . per primo

Prophecy

Out of the sea . . .
trees stripped of sails
lashing winds whipping up
halyards of mainsails and topping lifts
churning sea-foam
quiver   in walls.

It will be the helmsman
creature without a name
the man who fathoms
not death work
not submerged hull
that opens up gashed
to collapse . . . first

Stelle lontane

Nel palcoscenico
de lo spaziotempo
tutto incurva
a misura di un arco
succube della gravità
cui neanche la luce
può sfuggire

Ma qui . . . lontano dalle stelle
è tutto uno sgusciare
disattento
un chiacchiericcio
e il divenire sferza
l'arcuato profilo delle ossa
chiude fuori il sentire
di astri in movimento
nell'immenso stellare
che l'ampio vuoto
aduna

Distant Stars

On the stage
of spacetime
it all curves
in arc dimensions
under gravity's control
which not even light
can escape

But here . . . far from the stars
it's all just a distracted
worming out
a nattering
and what's in process of becoming
lashes against
the bowed contour of bones
closes out the sound
of astral bodies in movement
in the stellar immensity
that the vast emptiness
gathers

Lo Sciamano

Hanno tinto sulla mia colonna il verde vertebrale
della corteccia e il rosso sulla chioma
disperso fiori   raccolto frutti   acerbi
/della mancata maturazione mi devo ancora rassegnare/
I merli mi hanno preso come simbolo
nidificano all'ombra dei miei rami tra le fronde
riparo chiuso   protetto
cinguettano sul bianco della fronte
dicono che sono uno sciamano
perché di notte canto alla materia
madre   sostanza prima   attraente
non alla mente arida   inospitale

Ai loro occhi   guarniti di letizia
il mio tronco affollato è accogliente

Un attempato albero   sono diventato,
e i lombrichi strisciano tra le radici
in un continuo andare e ritornare
tra presente e passato

Il vomere affondato nei ricordi

Shaman

They painted my column the vertebral
bark green and the red of my mane
scatters flowers   I harvest fruit   that's tart
/I still need to resign myself to the fact it hasn't matured/
The blackbirds have taken me as a symbol
making nests in the shade among the leaves of my branches
closed refuge   protected
they twitter in the white of the forehead
they say I'm shaman
because at night I sing to   attractive
matter   mother   primary substance
not to the barren inhospitable   mind

In their eyes   decked-out in gladness
my jam-packed trunk is welcoming

I've turned into   an elderly tree
snails crawl along the roots
in a constant coming and going
between present and past

The ploughshare sunk into memories

Ricordanze

Le rane gracidavano sornione
e i pipistrelli   vere volpi volanti
si burlavano del latrare dei cani

Appena il buio avanzava dilatato
la chiarità della Luna
spazzava ansie e   paure

In un batter d'occhio
la memoria ricordava
tutti i nomi . . .
Per buona sorte anche gli
Innominabili

Recollections

Grumbling frogs would croak
and bats   real flying foxes
mocked the dogs' barking

As soon as creeping darkness took over
the Moon's clearness
cut through anxiety and   fears

In the blink of an eye
memory recalled
all the names . . .
For good luck   even
the Unspeakable

Narcissus poeticus

Stordisce . . . la neve d'aprile

Il giorno che mi presi sul serio
presi   fuoco di noia
e vennero pioggia e neve
e il rumore secco di stille
fra le falle di tegole che dalle travi
veniva giù sull'impiantito
insieme alle lacrime finché
il buffone che è in me
perse la mitezza e oscurando la voce
sgraziata   imbrattata di vino
schiuse l'uscio quasi a sfidare il cielo
aprendosi ai fulmini ariosi della follia

C'era il narciso da rianimare
un attimo prima che di gelo   morisse

Narcissus poeticus

April snow . . .   numbs

The day I took myself seriously
I took on   boredom fire
the result was rain and snow
and sound dry with drops
in the cracks between the shingles
falling from beams onto
the floor together with tears
until the Fool that's in me
lost mildness   the grating voice
stained with wine   darkening
the door opened up almost like a challenge to the heavens
an opening for lunacy's airy lightning

There was a narcissus to reanimate
one second before freezing   to death

Il sette passi(il serpente)

Fra rami giaciglio s'inarca
il sette passi, dilatando le costole
corpo verde e marrone
lo stesso colore delle mangrovie
Se almeno avessi il suo sguardo intimidatorio
gli occhi color bronzo
il morso che non lascia scampo

Bacia la terra la sua pelle corteccia
che al sole risplende

Quante volte ho provato ad essere prudente
come il serpente
quante volte mimetizzato ho percorso anfibio
la via della parola
  con interruzione e continuità
strisciando al suolo
stordito quasi privo
di vita

Siete pasos (snake)

Siete pasos it winds among a bed
of branches, raising its spine
its body green and brown
same color as the mangroves
If only I had its threatening stare
the bronze color of its eyes
the bite with no way out.

Its bark skin kisses earth
dazzles with the sun's light.

How many times I've tried to be wary
like the snake,
how many times amphibian I've travelled
camouflaged along the road of words
with interruption and continuity
creeping along the ground in a daze
almost lifeless

L'Arcolaio

L'ordito a piombo e nel passo
la spoletta volante insinua
un filo ad ogni trama
coricato battuto pressato
nel cangiante cedevole tessuto

Ad ogni trama ad ogni passo
tortuoso la sua navetta cade
nella rete ben tesa
vero intreccio di nodi
ricamata con aghi dalla punta
rovente scende sui grandi occhi
di donna rosso sangue ancorati al telaio

E non basta che sia d'oro l'arcolaio
per dipanare la matassa
per riavvolgere questo tempo avaro
della sua vita   in un gomitolo

The Spinning Wheel

The warp perpendicular and in the shed
the flying shuttle inserts
a thread into every weaving
flat hit and pressed against
in the supple color-changing fabric

With every weave and with every tortuous
shed its shuttle falls
taut into the net
real twisted knots
needle-worked with needles with scorching
point coming down blood-red on the great eyes
of women anchored to loom.

And even if the spinning wheel were made gold
it wouldn't be enough to untangle the skein
to rewind this mingy time of
her life   in a ball.

Galatea

Schiumano desideri
per la gioia
dei delfini in amore
Ai tuoi piedi
ho deposto collane,
pendenti di perle e raccolto gigli
di mare rami di mirto e agrumi
Impazzire è un gioco di vene
che pulsano
labbra che premono
sulla bocca e sul seno
Perdo la ragione   la notte
quando ti stringo
e sei tu conchiglia in amore a scatenare
la mia follia
Nove volte la Luna
ha compiuto il suo cerchio
e tu non rispondi più
  ai miei baci
Mi sembra di toccare
qualcosa di freddo
cera che solidifica
candela troppe volte riaccesa
Ma è all'alba dell'ultimo giorno
che t'ho vista mutare
tramutare nel marmo
di una statua

Ed ora amo una . . . statua

Galatea

Desires are churning
and foaming for the joy
of dolphins in love.
I laid necklaces and pearl
pendants at your feet
and I gather sea lilies
myrtle and citrus branches
Going mad is a game where veins
throb
lips push
against mouth and breast
I lose my mind   at night
when I grip you
and you are a shell in love setting off
my insanity
The Moon has made its circle
nine times
and you no longer
  respond to my kisses
It feels like I'm touching
something cold
solidified wax
a candle re-lit too many times
It's dawn of the last day
when I see you changing
transforming into the marble
of a statue

And now I love . . . a statue

Le Sabbie del tempo

Il ruvido pugnale del tempo nel tuo cuore hai spinto per essere
immortale mia bella Kaileena dagli occhi di perla E'
tua l'azzurra clessidra con fine sabbia dorata il
solo scrigno capace di contenerla Per me
nessuna magia Io non possiedo
la maschera che il tempo
rallenta

e

neppure
il bastone con la testa
di serpente che vorticando la
sabbia può rimescolarlo placare la tempesta
Sono vecchio Kaileena e disperatamente cerco di
trattenerti di legarti al presente all'unico evanescente
labile consistente tempo nell'umbratile limbo dell'esistente

The Sands of time

You have thrust the jagged dagger of time into your heart
to be immortal my beautiful Kaileena with pearl eyes
Your hourglass with the fine golden sand
is the only treasure chest that can
contain it No magic for me
I myself do not possess
the mask that time
shrinks
and
not even
the staff with serpent
head agitating the sand can
shake it up and calm the storm I'm
old Kaileena and desperately trying to keep you
here to bind you to the present of the only evanescent
unstable consistent time in the umbratile limbo of the living

da I QUADERNI DELL'USSERO

from NOTEBOOKS FROM THE USSERO

Avatar

Gole latrano
di mostri   vampe
dalla bocca nessun umidore
nella notte si rovesciano a mordere
esseri vestiti di giallo colore delle divinità
solari deliberate a reincarnarsi negli uomini-leone
sulla fronte regali corone cangianti piume penne di pavone
numi incapaci di risalire il fiume incavato nel ventre della terra
inadeguati a ristabilire l'ordine universale mettere in fuga novelli Avatar
i mostri che alimentano il falso sentire le cattive abitudini dell'intelletto il degrado
che appesta ad omnes gradus   l'Umanità

Avatar

barking
throats of monsters
blazes from the mouth at night
spills into eats into no trace of humidity
creatures clothed in yellow color of sun gods intent
on reincarnating as lion-men regal crowns iridescent plumage
peacock feather on the forehead deities incapable of returning to river hollowed
out within the earth's bowels inadequate for reestablishing universal order to put to flight
all reborn Avatars the monsters feeding false feeling the mean habits of intellect degradation
plaguing omnes gradus   Humanity

Disvelàrsi

Chiedersi come . . .
l'aggirarsi di nuvole
lente
possa togliere visibilità
alle montagne
occultarne il profilo
immutabile
avvolgerle come forma del tutto
che cessa di mostrarsi
allo sguardo
spiraglio che si apre
sul mondo
Le cose finite
non appaiono
in questo ritorno nel nulla
  in questo non essere più
Al loro dileguarsi io brindo
fino . . . all'annichilimento

Removing the veil

Ask yourself . . .
how the slow
drifting of clouds
can take away
visibility
of mountains
conceal their unchangeable
contour
cover them like forms of every thing
that stops showing itself
to be seen
through a vent that opens
onto the world
In this return to nothing
in this no longer being
finite things
do not appear
To their dispersal I raise a glass
all the way to . . . annihilation

da PARTI DEL DISCORSO (POETICO)

from PARTS OF THE (POETIC) DISCOURSE

Acque sotto il cielo un solo luogo

Osservare impacciati naviplani
risalire fondali per mostrare
il mondo qual era
Acque sotto il cielo
un solo luogo
Segrete correnti riversano silenziose
argentei pesci dai quattro occhi sporgenti
Guizzano da mari levigati sulla terra informe
risorgive parvenze
Acque sotto il cielo
un solo luogo
suddiviso tra abisso e rive
di uno stesso perduto paradiso

Waters beneath the heavens one place alone

Observing ungainly flyingboats
rising from seafloors to show
what the world was
Waters beneath the heavens
one place alone
Secret currents once again pouring forth silent
silvery fish with four bulging eyes
They dart smooth from seas onto the shapeless earth
resurgent glimmerings
Waters beneath the heavens
one place alone
split between abyss and shores
of the same lost paradise

La Terra Promessa

Muore sulle barricate il mio tempo
nudo, come l'ailanto grigio cenere,
ha perso sgradevoli foglie, l'inverno
si veste del pallore dei muri,
l'indugio del merlo sul roseto esangue,
come se non avessi mai amato
il rosso struggente della rosa,
come se non avessi mai pianto,
quando alta si aggirava la musica
e guardinga   la poesia che le distanze colma
e si fa senso, per sondare l'ambiguo
raccapriccio della vita.
Lascia che sia   finita, che le voci
giungano assordite, che si pieghi a terra l'albero,
e si perdano gli occhi ad inseguire
la processione di formiche esultanti,
il tripudio dei vermi e dei bruchi
tutti in marcia verso la terra promessa.

The Promised Land

My time's dying on the barricades,
naked, like the ash gray ailanthus,
it's lost its ugly leaves, winter's
wearing the wall's pallor, the blackbird's
delay on the anemic rosebush,
as if I never loved
the rose's tormenting red,
as if I never cried
when music was turned up loud
and wary   poetry that closes distances
and disgusts,   in order to plumb
life's murky horrors.
Just let it be   over, let the voices
join together deaf, let the tree bend to the ground
and let the eyes go blind following
the parade of exultant ants,
the triumph of worms and grubs
all of them marching towards the promised land.

La Chiave

Mostra i denti la penombra,
incalza la chiave laconica,
sordo a quella stretta replica
il ventre grigio della serratura,
e una parte di urto da vita alla paura,
per intero ansima il pensiero.
L'altro lato gli ha lasciato intuire
l'esistenza di un mondo
destinato a rimanere in ombra.
Non può scorgerne l'invisibile bellezza
il corpo irresistibile,   attraente . . . ,
come un estraneo   si sente
irrimediabilmente   fuori,
assapora   come si sta
in una densa nuvola
di probabilità.

The Key

The half-light reveals teeth,
the reticent key closing in,
the lock's gray belly
deaf to that narrow repeating,
and one part of impact causes fears,
it entirely gasps thought.
The other side let it intuit
the existence of a world
destined to stay in shadow.
It can't glimpse the invisible beauty in it
the irresistible body,   attractive . . . ,
like a stranger   feels
irredeemably   outside,
savoring   what it's like being
in a dense cloud
of probability.

Come Furfanti

Come furfanti s'ammassano gli anni,
ma non sarà l'inverno, cupo e sciatto
a schiantarti il respiro.
Striscia il gatto tra i tuoi piedi nudi,
simula, sbadiglia, se ne distacca
per ritornarvi, lento.
Non sono gli arti il luogo
che il movimento avvolge, morbido, lieve.
Il luogo è il tempo, e sempre ti sorprende
l'idea di sottrarti arginando la vita,
la suggestione di esistere un attimo di più,
come se l'orditura dei giorni,
l'uno vicino all'altro, fitti, stipati,
possa farti dimenticare
che sarai tu a crollare, muso a terra,
dentro la cenere del mondo.

Same as Scoundrels

Same as scoundrels years get stashed
but it won't be grim and sloppy winter
snatching life.
The cat slinks between your naked feet
it feigns, it yawns, it pulls away
and comes back again, it's slow.
The limbs are not the place that's winded up
by the smooth light movement within it.
Place is time and you're always surprised
by the idea of syphoning from yourself to shore up your life,
by the attraction of existing one moment longer
as if the days' warp,
crammed, jam-packed one beside the other
can make you forget
that it will be you collapsing, snout to ground,
inside the ash of the world.

Il Paese

Lasciai valle colline compagni
alcuni destinati a compiere altrove
la propria avventura. Mai immaginavo
che sarei tornato io solo.
Il paese dorme ancora, qualche luce s'accende.
Da piccole fenditure figure note, impicciolite,
altre cancellate cominciano a rinsanguare la strade.
Anemia delle cose. Il fiume e' seccato, il ponte crollato,
e fatico a riconoscere la mia casa
come se l'istrice, solerte scavatore,
non scovasse più la sua tana.
Da quando vivo in cattività i miei aculei
si sono modificati,   spuntati,
Rispetto alla gente, al luogo, al tempo,
il disorientamento mi conduce, di volta in volta,
in un mondo apparente.
Qualche eco riaffiora così vengo riconosciuto,
si aprono vecchie ferite.
Uno mai visto prima, un demente, mi scorta al cimitero.
Lapidi strette le une alle altre, fiori anneriti, volti stanchi,
con alcuni eravamo cresciuti insieme.
Queste mura raggelano.
Alzo il bavero e lo sguardo oltre il filare dei cipressi.
Per capire ciò che realmente affiora
  i pensieri sempre più incapaci
  di significare il mondo.
Ma l'Oriente dov'è?

The Town

I left valleys hills friends
some of them destined to succeed
in their own adventures in other places. I never
imagined I'd return   the only one.
The town still sleeps, a few lights light up.
Through small slits recognizable figures, growing smaller,
others erased begin to infuse the street.
Anemia of things. The river's dried up, the bridge has
collapsed, and it's a struggle recognizing my house
as if the porcupine, diligent excavator
can no longer locate his lair.
Ever since I've lived in captivity my quills
have been modified   clipped,
As for people, place, time
disorientation guides me, from one condition to the next,
in an apparent world.
Some echoes return so I'm recognized,
old wounds open.
Someone not seen before, someone demented, escorts me to the
        cemetery.
Headstones crowded tightly together, blackened flowers, worn-
        out faces,
some of us grew up together.
These walls freeze.
I pull up my collar, stare beyond the row of cypress.
So as to understand what really makes thoughts
  resurface always more incapable
  of expressing the world.
Which way's the Orient, again?

E guardi il mare

E guardi il mare quieto, dall'alto, con occhi di gabbiano,
diffidente, da vicino lo vedi spumeggiare
di moti impercettibili, corpi minuti si confrontano,
divergono, s'infrangono, senza tregua, ora qua, ora là,
in ogni orientamento, in ogni dove, onde luccicanti
al sole come mosse da un vento invisibile che soffia
in superficie dove nulla permane di ciò che sull'acqua cammina.
Niente di sé conduce l'onda marina, solo l'eterno scivolare.
Non è un oggetto, non ha argomenti, la chiara identità
degli scogli, delle sabbie finissime.
E' solo un fluire di eventi, al pari del tuo corpo nudo
  fatto di incostanti molecole. E più l'onda s'appressa,
più l'animo trascende l'attimo appena vissuto,
prima di sciogliersi, nuovamente, in mare.
Chiedersi se la mente sia la rada dove ammarano
i gabbiani, il porto che si lascia crudelmente insabbiare
da voci rauche, grevi sentimenti in un solo pensiero.
Ecco perché il mondo temi oltre la boa, oltre l'azzurro
profondo, il fosco remigare, l' illusorio orizzonte.

And you look at the sea

And you look at the sea, quiet, from above, with seagull eyes,
diffident, from close up you see it foam
with imperceptible movements, minute bodies clashing with each
        other,
splitting off, breaking off, no truce, now here, now there,
in every orientation, in every place, sparkling waves
in sunlight as if they were being moved by an invisible wind
        blowing
on surfaces where nothing remains of what walks on water.
Nothing in itself directs the sea waves, only the eternal slide.
Clear identity of the cliffs, of the finest sands,
it is not an object, it has no arguments,
it is only a flow of events, like your naked body
  made up of unstable molecules. And the closer the wave
        approaches,
the more the soul transcends the just-lived moment,
before being released, once again, into the sea.
Ask yourself if the mind is the roadstead where seagulls
land, the port where raucous voices and the oppressive
feeling in one single thought are cruelly left to silt.
That's why you fear the world beyond the buoy, beyond the
        deepest
blue, rowing in gloom, illusive horizon.

Formiche

Nel breve periodo tutte erano in vita.
Non vive veramente.
Vive nell'indifferenza.
A nessuno veniva in mente di dar loro un nome.
Sconosciute anche a se stesse.
E nemmeno inducevano alla tenerezza.
E non sapevano fino a quando avrebbero goduto
del beneficio di esistere.
Poi le cose sono accadute.
E non hanno fatto in tempo ad echeggiare,
prima di franare nell'oblio
E non ci vuole tanta scaltrezza per indovinare
in quale alba erano nate, e quale notte le ha lasciate
affondare fra le fredde fessure della terra.

Continui ad illuderti sino alla fine, sedotto dall'essere
un nume o un cigno, che incruento sia il tragitto,
spietato, verso il nulla.

Ants

For a short time they were all living.
Not really living.
Living in indifference.
It didn't occur to anyone to give names.
Each was unknown even to itself.
And they didn't even arouse compassion.
And they didn't know how long they would enjoy
the benefits of existing.
Then things happened.
And the bells didn't go off in time
before their landslide into oblivion.
And you don't have to be clever to guess
which dawn they were born into, and which night let them
fall between the earth's cold crevices.

You keep deluding yourself right to the end, seduced by being
a deity or a swan, that the crossing is going to be bloodless,
with no mercy, towards nothingness.

Quasi mai

Quasi mai ho scritto col sangue.
un limite, forse, un rinvio,
non un disimpegno.
Mai un graffito,
lo schianto di un urlo sui muri,
quando il cielo s'imbratta di lingue rosso sangue,
E mi chiedi come ciò sia potuto accadere
a un animo desto, in testa le passioni,
lo sdegno che sfigura,
l' ira che irrompe e dura,
donne vessate, violate, assassinate.
E sono insorto.
Mai col sangue però,
quello che a gocce cola
da squarci di pugnali
per i quali, senza lamento,
morirò   domani.

Almost Never

I almost never wrote in blood.
a limit, perhaps, a postponement,
not non-committed.
Never scratch-work,
the torment of screaming against walls,
when the sky is smeared in blood-red tongues,
And you ask me how that could have happened
to an alert soul, with suffering at the forefront,
outrage disfiguring it,
rage that bursts in and stays,
women harassed, raped, assassinated.
And I am rebellious.
But never with blood,
the kind in drops that filters
from gashes from daggers
from which, without complaint,
I'll die   tomorrow.

Isole

Tutto lo spazio reca l'Assenza.
Ombre sui libri.
Nemmeno Shakespeare riluce.
Qui
non si nomina dio.

Sono estraneo, io,
a tutti, a tutto.

Fuori piove a dirotto,
ed io sto diventando
un' Isola.

Islands

All space carries Absence.
Shadows on books.
Not even Shakespeare shines bright.
Right here
god isn't named.

I am extraneous, I,
to everyone, to everything.

Outside it's raining buckets,
and I'm turning into
an Island.

Gli incomodi pensieri

Gli incomodi pensieri ho spedito
lontano dalla vista, che tra i sensi
fruisce del più ampio raggio,
oltre lo spazio che tutto avvolge,
oltre l'aria greve, opprimente,
per sentirmi redento, libero
di meditare su ciò che mi attende.

Ma anche il meno inquietante
al suo rivelarsi, quello più fuggevole
e vago, non fa che ripresentarsi.

Tutti! Tutti sono tornati
per farmi diventare   Cieco.

Inconvenient Thoughts

I've sent inconvenient thoughts far away
out of sight, so the more expansive ray
can get full benefit among the senses,
beyond the space everything's wrapped up in
beyond the heavy, oppressive, air,
so I can feel redeemed, and free
to meditate about whatever it is that concerns me.

But even the least disturbing
in its revealing, that one most evasive
and vague, is able only to represent itself.

Every one of them! Every one of them returned
to make me go   Blind.

Girasoli

La meridiana luce riveste di eccessivo ardore
l'astuta moltitudine dei girasoli,
lo stelo dritto fino al crepuscolo,
inchiodato ognuno alla sua zolla di terra.
L'ora in cui appare la paura
che si raffreddi l'ardente vita.
L'esistente riaffiora dai clamori di un tempo,
intermittenti languori, la logorante intesa
di non parlarne prima della resa
che si consuma con servili mestizie.

Le povere consumate notizie di me stesso.

Sunflowers

The noonday sun covers the astute multitude
of sunflowers in an excessive ardor,
stem straight right up until twilight,
each one planted into its little clump of earth.
The hour in which the fear
that the ardent life will chill appears.
Those that exist resurface from the din of time,
intermittent languors, the exhausting arrangement
to not speak of it before the rendering
that consumes with a servile mournfulness.

The pitiful consumed news of my self.

A capo chino

A capo chino, come un'abitudine,
tra vecchi caseggiati, luoghi abitati
da ombre rigide, ti sfiorano, nessuna
che si distingua.
Non avverti, nei vicoli, la distanza
dei passi che dentro vi risuonano,
ovunque ti inabissi, in disparte,
dopo aver condiviso l'odore dei bistrò
che attanaglia la gola.

Che tu voglia soffermarti o no,
gli altri, avvisi, del tuo passare,
soltanto per soliloqui.

Head Hanging

Head hanging, like a habit,
among old housing complexes, places inhabited
by rigid shadows; they graze you, not one of them
distinguishable.
No warning in these alleys
of the distance in the steps echoing there
anywhere you sink, off to the side,
after having partaken in the aroma of the bistros
that has your throat in a clutch.

Whether or not you want to stop
others, warned, about your passing through
even just in soliloquies.

Lola

Giace sull'arenile l' amuleto
carpito alla roccia madre.
Libero, a suo senno, potrà incendiare
il cielo, ardere le foreste, proteggere l'amore
armonizzante. Più di quante virtù vanta il monile,
più grazioso, attraente, il collo della donna
che indossa l'ambra gialla.
Splende, al confronto, la sua supremazia,
avvincente, sensuale, voluttuosa,
abile a destreggiarsi, troppo pericolosa
per uomini vulnerabili, docili, arrendevoli,
come me.

Lola

Wrested from mother rock
the amulet lies upon the shore.
Free by his own will, it can set the sky
on fire, set forests ablaze, protecting harmonizing
love. The necklace shows off the virtues above and beyond
of a neck beyond delicate, beyond attractive, of the woman
who wears the yellow amber.
Her absorbing, sensual, voluptuous
superiority, by comparison, shines,
capable of maneuvering, much too dangerous,
for vulnerable, docile, malleable men,
like me.

Doppelgänger

L'altro me stesso, da cui dissento spesso,
ha sobillato tutti i miei io con la pretesa
di impormi la resa.
Dentro di me c'è un grande eccitamento,
ognuno vuole vivere a casaccio,
e le vorrò vedere le anime ribelli,
le felici,le truci, le bugiarde traditrici,
  anime errabonde, piene d'ombre, vanitose
spose di famelici lupi,
fronteggiare i dirupi nella casa fermaglio . . .

Mi ruba il sonno la vergogna
d'esser messo alla gogna.
L'abbaglio di averle dominate.
Nate con me, più scaltre di me stesso,
mi mandano in congedo (spero nella fine incruenta)
come fossi un arredo in disuso, dismesso.

E' giunta l'alba che la notte addenta,
a poco a poco il buio decolora,
che vadano in malora.

Doppelgänger

My other myself, from which I often dissent,
stirs up all my selves under the pretense
of ordering my surrender.
There's great excitement inside me,
with each of them wanting to live haphazardly,
and I will want to see them, rebel souls,
content souls,the cruel ones, the traitorous liars,
  the drifter souls dense with shadows, ostentatious
brides of ravenous wolves,
facing the cliff faces inside the clasp house . . .

My sleep is stolen by shame
and put in stockades,
The error of having controlled them.
Born with me, even shrewder than my self,
they put me on leave (I hope for the soft ending)
as if I were an unused, cast-off, piece of furniture.

With night nibbling away dawn has arrived,
darkness is bleaching out bit by bit,
so they can go bad.

Ho quasi consumato

Ho quasi consumato
la materia di cui sono fatto
ricadrò in avanti
o all'indietro
dopo aver compiuto
il massimo tragitto
fortemente curvato
sprofonderò su di me
crollerò sotto il peso delle mie ossa
e non potrò sfuggire
nulla di me potrà uscire
da quella porta si può solo entrare
neppure la luce
di cui erano fatti i miei occhi
uscirà
non ha sufficiente
velocità
per sottrarsi all'attrazione
esiziale
il tempo stesso rallenterà
il suo corso
fino ad arrestarsi
qualcuno di quelli che hanno ruotato
accanto a me
prossimi all'azzurra sfera
dei miei sogni
scorterà ciò che ho soltanto immaginato
ospiterà il mio presente

I have almost consumed

I have almost consumed
the material I'm made of
I'll fall forward again
or backwards
after having finished
the greatest crossing
greatly curved over
I'll cave in on myself
I'll collapse under the weight of my bones
and I won't be able to escape
nothing of me will be able to leave
you can only enter through that door
not even the light
my eyes were made with
will get out
it doesn't have enough
velocity
to extract itself from the fatal
attraction
time itself will slow
its course
until it stops
some of those who spun
near me
near the blue sphere
of my dreams
it will escort what I have only imagined
it will play host to my present

il mio passato
dentro la propria sfera
verso il suo verde
lontano
personale
futuro

my past
inside its own sphere
near its own green
distant
personal
future

Arno

A Percy Shelley

Clamori di gocce che i larghi fianchi
sfiorano per nutrirsi d'ossigeno

Sul greto grigio incombono verità
come rughe del volto che si specchia
in acque chiare dove cavalli scalzi
abbeverano le fronti umide, e strette chiglie,
da un medesimo vento sospinte,
costeggiano pigramente le rive.

Ho affittato una barca per scoprire,
alla foce, quale mare, seppure sconvolto,
mi darà il vantaggio di decidere
se invertire la rotta,o perdermi
dove muore il fiume, nell'infinita   disventura.

Arno

In a frenzy the broad flanks are skimming
drops to feed themselves with oxygen

Truth looms over the gray pebble river bank
like creases in a face
reflecting in clear waters where unshod horses
wet foreheads, and keels straight-up
from the same wind sighing,
indolently approach the shores.

I rented a boat to discover,
even if upended, which sea, at its mouth,
will give me the advantage of deciding
whether to change course or lose myself
where the river dies, in the infinite   mishap.

Ruotare attorno ad una stella

Ruotare attorno ad una stella
pianeta di luce sospesa
abbandonando il punto, l'origine.
Dentro l'arcobaleno si vive
di un tepore sottile,
coscienza nuova che imprime
nuova vita, l'amore.
Lo sento l'amore all'ombra
delle cinque lune, tenui
luminosità sulla pelle, nuove
possibilità.
Nuove intenzioni.
movimento, cambiamento.
Attorno, ruotare attorno . . .
Nella realtà,   nulla accade,
niente in quel punto, in quel giorno
fissato   per il mio ritorno.

Rotate around a star

Rotate around a star
planet of suspended light
abandoning point, origin.
One lives inside the rainbow
of a faint warmth
new consciousness imprinting
new life, love.
I sense love in the shadows
of the five moons, tenuous
luminosities on the skin, new
possibilities.
New intentions.
movement, change.
Around, turn around . . .
In reality,   nothing occurs,
nothing at that point, on that day
set   for my return.

La volta che

La volta che la fiamma si accese
nei miei occhi una fiocina tutto fuoco,
sfuggita alle nubi più dense,
punta arroventata lucente,
colpì il mio aquilone sul punto di volare.
Il frastuono non mi lasciò costruire una ragione,
sulla stessa scia del tuono una nuova saetta,
un nuovo strepitio, verso il suolo, verso di me

Fulminea nello stesso luogo
apparve una figura posta tra terra e cielo.
In quella intravidi una donna.
La spiavo con gli occhi dell'amore,
sguardi come fossero mani, fluide ardenti infuocate.
L'impulso travolgente mi faceva esultare,
gioire acutamente.
L'alchimia dei magici alambicchi
cercavo di richiamare a me, e . . . . . . avevo
la follia giusta per renderla visibile . . e . . . . possibile.

The time that

The time that the flame ignited
in my eyes, a harpoon all fire
escaped the densest clouds,
glowing red-hot point,
he struck my kite at the point of take-off.
The thundering did not permit me to construct a rationale,
on the same wake of thunder a new bolt of lightning,
a new din, near the ground, near me.

In that same location, like lightning,
a figure appeared positioned between earth and the heavens.
I glimpsed a woman in it.
I spied her with love in my eyes,
with looks like flowing, burning, inflamed hands.
An overwhelming impulse caused me to exult,
to rejoice piercingly.
Alchemy of magic alembics
I tried to summon her to me, and . . . . . . I had
just the right lunacy for making her visible . . and . . . . feasible.

Tutto ci avvolge in un unico sguardo

La matita come spada sanguigna
a fendere il nostro sentire, e noi stessi,
lo stesso istinto in un'estate torrida se l'idea
incombe sui nostri attraversamenti per incitare
arterie e vene, che non sanno sottrarsi
all'urto, e si lasciano invadere per il tempo esiguo
che irrompe il nuovo avvertire.
L' immerso fuori da sé, la visione mancante.
E tutto diviene un impasto di fibre e fuoco,
dicibile e indicibile.
Un varco appena percettibile ignorato
chissà da quanto,
un pensiero modificante che trasfigura
struttura e mente.
Un solo istante per trovarsi ed esistere
Tutto ci avvolge in un unico sguardo.

Everything's enclosed within one look

Pencil as blood-red sword
cleaving our feelings,   and ourselves,
same instinct in a sweltering summer if idea
threatens our street crossings, inciting
arteries and veins, and they don't know how to back out
of clash, and they let themselves be taken
over   by interrupting time slivers   warning anew.
Lost outside yourself, vision gone.
And everything becomes a jumble of fiber and flame,
sayable and unsayable.
A barely perceptible gap unseen
who knows for how long
an altering thought transfiguring
structure and mind.
One single moment to find oneself and to exist
Everything's enclosed within one look.

Galileo

Mai che venisse meno   la magia,
quando occhi minuscoli indagavano
spazi   sfavillanti di atomi.
Un palpitare   di stelle   lucenti,
volteggi di crisalidi succinte,
lo stupore,   il senso di mistero,
vagheggiavo,   grazie   a te.
al tuo occhio gigante,   lo sguardo
sicuro, distante, compresi   l'immanente
geometria del creato, nuove profezie,   l'inaspettato.

Tu   che distanze stellari misuravi lunghe anni luce
liberando   il mondo   dalla costrizione.
Tu   che mettevi in gioco   la tua vita
per una stella nuova, decisa a dileguarsi,
  e a ripresentarsi, la prova di un mutabile universo
che la ragione scosse,   e grande   apparve   il disegno
di cui parte   io sono   grato a te,
la sensata esperienza che promuove
l'amore   per la verità.
Solo   per questo   amore,   profondo,
serbo   la parola, la coscienza   camuffa
  la paura   del divenire, placa
la baruffa   dei sensi,   abiura   lo spavento.

Galileo

Magic   never shrank
when miniscule eyes investigated
spaces   sparking with atoms.
A pulsing   of lucid   stars,
spins of concise chrysalises,
astonishment,   the sense of mystery,
thanks   to you   i wandered
in your giant eye, the sure
distant eye, I understood   the immanent
geometry of creation, new prophecies,   the unexpected.

You who measured stellar distances long light years
liberating   the world   from constraint.
You who put your life   to the test
for one new star, determined to disperse,
  and in presenting again, the proof of a changeable universe
that reason shocks,   and the great design
of which its part   appeared   I am grateful to you,
for the sensate experience that promotes
love   of truth.
Only   because of this   profound,   love,
do I bear   words, conscience   fear
  camouflaged   in the becoming, brawling
senses   calmed, recanted   does it frighten me.

POESIE INEDITE

UNPUBLISHED POEMS

Preludio

Brevità dello spazio scenico
la luce si posa su una nicchia
buio su tutto il resto fa spazio il silenzio
vuoto
A nessuna porta il ruolo cardine
Si schiude lo scrigno in cui il passato perdura
Le resurrezioni di Proust recuperate
foss'anche per un attimo
Oltre i confini di scena
inconsapevole l'organista
a quello scampanellio
sovrappone la musica di Bach
sfida il vuoto e lo spazio
toccata e fuga in re minore 565
alta volteggia da una parte all'altra
Che cosa pensi   adesso?
Che farai del buio commediante struccato?
Immagina che tutto si concluda con un accordo
Immagina che l'emozione cresca
e qualcosa in te si accenda
Avrai una parte da rappresentare
dopotutto . . .
Immagino che accada veramente

[Ma] è solo un Eco
quel che ne resta
pian piano
si spegne

Prelude

Concision of the scene's space
light settles over the dark niche
empty silence
makes space everywhere else
No door to the leading role
It opens the treasure chest on the past that persists
The recovered resurrections of Proust
if only for an instant
Beyond the confines of the scene
the organist
unaware
of this pealing
superimposes the music of Bach
defying the dark and the space
toccata and fugue in d minor 565
circling high from one part to another
What do you think   now?
What will you do with the dark comedian with no make-up?
Imagine it all ends in an agreement
Imagine emotion builds
and something in you lights up
You'd have a part to play
after all . . .
I imagine it really will happen.

[But] it's only an Echo
that remains of it
little by little
it fades away

Il dipinto e la realtà

Deluso dalle imitazioni, belle figure, luoghi ordinari,
forme, colori per niente naturali, un di fuori che ti assale,
fatto di segni che lo spazio modella con emozione lirica.
Il dipinto è meno di quanto si manifesta nella Natura.
Nessuna cosa è più viva di quel puntino rosso che brilla là,
nell'angolo grigio della stanza, o di quella porta
che potrebbe aprirsi, ad un tratto.
Che ti salta in mente di rivelare certe cose in poesia?
Nel silenzio si sente un tic-tac ordigno ad orologeria.
E' il cuore.
Stranamente ha tre uscite questa stanza,
una celata dalla specchiera dà verso l'esterno,
il vuoto e lo specchio che ti guardano,
che ti scoprono la faccia, denudano la maschera
se dalla feritoia si infiltra il tenue azzurro cielo.
Che cosa altro pretendi di vedere da una finestra?
Cos'altro vuoi che appaia ancora?
La tragicità della vita si nasconde dietro l'immagine
più misteriosa e lieta. Brilla, qui, in primo piano
l'astro di Thérèse vista di spalle che indossa
la robe rose a strisce verticali argentate e un tablier noir,
lo sguardo in direzione delle case, non degli alberi
che Bazille ritrae in secondo piano.
Dramma della quiete, della serenità.

Painting and Reality

Disillusioned by imitations, good impressions, common places,
forms, colors not the least bit natural, a kind that accosts you
    from outside,
made of signs that space shapes with lyric emotion.
Painting is less than what is revealed in Nature.
No thing is more alive than that small red dot sparkling right
    there,
in the gray corner of the room, or than that door
which might open, all of a sudden.
What leaps to your mind to reveal certain things in poetry?
In the silence there's the sound of a clockworks.tic-tick
    contraption.
It's the heart.
Oddly enough, this room has three exits,
the one hidden by the mirror on the wall leads outside,
emptiness and mirror watching you,
where they reveal your face, if the pale blue sky
penetrates from the opening they strip off the mask.
What else do you expect to see from a window?
What else do you need to appear once more?
Life's tragicality hides behind the most mysterious
and content image. It glimmers, here, in the foreground,
Thérèse's star seen from behind where
she's wearing the pink dress with silvery vertical stripes and a
    tablier noir
gaze in the direction of the houses, not the trees
which Bazille depicts in the background.
Quiet drama, of serenity.

Sembra essere proprio questa la realtà.
La figura virtuale rimanda all'esistente.
Dove è dunque la poesia?
E' nel modo con cui si divide lo sguardo
tra lo spazio racchiuso dalla cornice, Thérèse, colori, ombre,
o le cose viste nella coscienza della luce azzurra
che manifesta l'astronomia del cielo in una piccola camera?
Ma non è lì che ti senti testimone, spettatore gettato,
dimenticato bagliore di un Sole già crudelmente
tramontato.

It seems reality really is just this.
The virtual figure postpones the existing one.
Where then is poetry?
Is it in the way one splits the gaze
between the frame's enclosed space, Thérèse, colors, shadows,
or the things seen in the consciousness of the blue light
revealing the sky's astronomy inside a small room?
But it's not there where you feel a witness, ejected spectator,
forgotten glow of a Sun already cruelly
set.

Françoise

Nome da non evocare apertamente,
sottrarlo alla vigilanza della ballerina russa,
uscita di senno pour l'amour fou.
Non deve esser percepito, che non venga avvertito
il linguaggio, scenico, compreso il grido di stupore
nello spazio entro cui tutto accade,
sullo sfondo d'un café dans la capitale française,
la figura in lontananza si avvicina come un suono,
sempre sul punto di vibrare o svanire,
e lascia in sospeso qualcosa di ammaliante.
Il corpo sinuoso anima il desiderio
dell'anziano artista, creatore e distruttore.
Sinfonia di forma, colore, *lo sguardo rosso* ardente
come il vestito e i capelli a paggio, negli occhi belli,
che avvinsero anche Matisse, primeggia una luce audace.
Cos'è quel suono che si sente?
Il vento fra gli alberi del boulevard rende musicale l'attesa.
Ha vent'anni Françoise, pittrice cubista,
un esegete delle moderne peinture.
La natura, parola di Hermann Hesse, non si getta
nelle braccia del primo venuto, così come l'arte e la sapienza.
Vivono nel paradiso dell'amore, noi nell'aridità,
strimpella il suonatore cieco di chitarra. Non sa
che quella donna è destinata ad essere ornamento,
musa ispiratrice, sposa avvenente.
Fuori dalla piccola finestra aperta, quasi a terra,

Françoise

Name not to invoke openly,
to extract it from the surveillance of the russian ballerina,
out of her mind pour l'amour fou.
It doesn't have to be sensed, because scenic
language is not about to given any warnings, including the cry
of astonishment in the space where it all happens,
in the backdrop of a café dans la capitale française,
the figure in the distance approaches like a sound,
always on the point of vibrating or dissipating,
and it leaves something enthralling hanging.
The sinuous body animates desire
in the old artist, creator, and destroyer .
Symphony of form, color, red eyes like fire,
like the dress and hair of a pageboy cut, in beautiful eyes,
it captivated even Matisse, an audacious light catches the eye.
What is that sound one hears?
The wind through the trees in the boulevard made the wait
	musical.
Françoise, cubist painter, is twenty years old,
an interpreter of modern painting.
Nature, in Hermann Hesse's word, doesn't throw itself
into the arms of the first one to come along like art and wisdom
	do.
They live in the paradise of love, we in aridness,
the blind guitar player strums. He does not know
that woman is destined to become ornament,
inspiring muse, attractive bride.
Outside the small open window, nearly at ground level,

giungono i profumi a riempire l'aria della stanza,
l'amore è la cornice entro cui isolarsi,
ma il celebre ospite infrange, impunemente,
l'antico legame tra donna e natura.
— Ad ogni successione dovrei bruciare la donna
precedente, così me ne libererei . . . —
Questa volta fu Lei, demone e dea, a lasciarlo,
a frantumare l'orgoglio del genio, la sua presunzione.
Lei che dipinge al centro le sue tazzine da caffè,
le costringe in quei colori chiari e quel celeste e verde;
il marrone-viola del piano risuona nel contrasto,
il giallo sullo sfondo, o quando stende il rosso cadmio
tonalità dominante nel verde base della tela.

Vai pure avanti tu per la tua via, Françoise Gilot.
Non farai la fine delle altre regine /della sua vita/.
Si appese al collo Marie Thérèse, Jacqueline
si sparò un colpo di pistola in testa,
Ol'ga e Dora persero la ragione.
Moi seulement, je suis . . . encore en vie — grida Françoise.

scents arrive to fill the air in the room,
love is the frame in which we isolate ourselves,
but the famous guest shatters the ancient bonds
between woman and nature with impunity.
—With each new one I would have to burn the last
woman so that I could liberate myself . . . —
This time it was Her, demon and goddess, to leave him,
to shatter the pride of the genius, and his presumption.
Her. She paints its coffee cups at the center of the picture.
restricting them to those clear colors and in that sky blue and
    green;
the purple-brown of the plane echoes in the contrast,
the yellow in the background, or as the cadmium red
extends dominant tonality in the green   base of the canvas.
Go forward with your life, Françoise Gilot.

Do not have the ending of the other queens /in his life/.
Marie Thérèse hanged herself, Jacqueline
shot herself in the head with a pistol,
Ol'ga and Dora lost their minds.
Moi seulement, je suis . . . encore en vie—Françoise cries.

A Max Frisch

Mare e cielo adunati in un unico sguardo,
visione maestosa, sublime. Ritta sullo scoglio
una minuscola figura, si toglie il cappello
alzandolo il più possibile per sventolarlo.
E non ci sono vele all'orizzonte, angoli ristretti, relitti,
solo stupore, a Palavas, con cui riempirsi gli occhi,
ebbrezza che in un uomo ordinario sparisce.
Non in Courbet. Fierezza, monumentalità,
unisce a quella solitudine, della sua luce
penetra il mondo che si schiude al modo di uno scrigno
e ha bisogno della luce del mondo per esistere.
Nel retroterra un uomo è diventato pietra.
Medusa non l'ha guardato, chissà perché è impietrito
e a che fine le ombre s'intrecciano sul capo anguicrinito,
quale identità lui che, forse, ha conosciuto
molti luoghi in cui fermarsi per rendersi invisibile.
Chi è? Ha forse consumato per intero il respiro?
Lo spazio intorno trasfigura per la rapidità
con cui sfilano tram, un continuo va e vieni.
Uomini che si muovono come nuvole incombenti,
senza avvertire d'essere anelli di una catena casuale,
e persistono ancora . . . a passare. Forme dissolventi.
Pura casualità l'incontro. L'altro non deve tornare,
prendere una via, ripartire all'istante:
"Non stavi per caso fuggendo dalla sventura?
Per quasi tutto il tempo della vita io l'ho sfuggita

To Max Frisch

Sea and sky convened in a single look,
sublime, mighty vision. A miniscule figure
upright on the cliff, he takes off his hat
and raises it as high as he can to wave it.
And there aren't any sails, or narrow angles, wrecks
on the horizon, just amazement, in Palavas, so that your eyes
flood, an ecstasy that in an ordinary
man disappears. Not in Courbet. Fineness, monumentality,
combined with that solitude its light penetrating the world which
     it
opens like a treasure chest, and it needs the world's light for
     existing.
In the hinterland a man turned to stone.
Medusa didn't look at him, who knows why he petrified
and why the shadows were weaving together over his
eelyhorsehair head, which identity he'd known, perhaps,
the many places he'd stopped to keep himself invisible.
Who is he? Perhaps he took up all the air?
Surrounding space transfigures from the rapidity
with which trams pull away, a constant coming and going.
Men moving like looming clouds,
without warning of its being links in random sequence,
and still they perist . . . to pass through. Dissolving forms.
The encounter, pure randomness. The other doesn't have a
     return,
taking one road, taking off again immediately.
"Weren't you trying to escape misfortune?
I've fled for almost an entire lifetime

riducendomi in solitudine."

Amnesia di esseri e luoghi.

Agli uomini comuni poco è concesso di chiedere, o sapere,
arduo trarre inferenze, deduzioni.

Immagini indurite, alterate, confuse con quelle di altri.

Quei peli di un rosso chimico slavati, gli occhi azzurri
iniettati di ruggine, l'arcata inferiore sporgente,
sulla fronte appena percettibile il segno di una cicatrice.

Il tempo estatico dell'insurrezione delirante
ti può esplodere in faccia, auto-annientare, come l'esaltazione
di Courbet per la Comune, pagata a caro prezzo.

Nessuna espressione, ansia di abbandonare le tenebre,
persiste la storica immobilità.

E quel suono alto nell'aria? Un nuovo espediente?

Solleva il Quartetto per Archi l'alto sentire, l'Opera 132,
quanto di più solenne e impenetrabile ci sia nel Genio,
afflitto da ipoacusia. Musica, tempo di redenzione, dell'utopia.

Nessuno che sia disposto ad accoglierla.

Nessuno che sappia congiungersi con Beethoven.

Suoni, segni, e note, alte in numero sempre minore,
condurranno a un raggiro.

L' assurdità è che uno ha coscienza della propria vuotezza
e l'altro, annichilito, non ha un'identità.

Ma se nella tasca interna della sua giacca scovate un biglietto,
solo andata, per Amsterdam,
Signori, non dubitate quell'uomo sono io.

reducing myself in solitude."
Amnesia of beings and places.
Little in asking or to knowing is granted to common men,
it's arduous hauling inferences and deductions.
Images harden and change, confused with those of others.
Those skins of a washed-out red chemist with blue eyes,
injected with rust, lower jaw jutting out,
trace of a barely visible scar on the forehead.
The ecstatic time of delirious insurrection
can explode in your face, self-annihilating, like Courbet's
exaltation for the Comune, heavy price.
No expression, anxiety over abandoning darknesses,
the historical immovabilility endures.
And that sound up in the air? A new expedient?
The String Quartet lifts up the noble mind, Opus 132,
the most solemn and impenetrable that here is of the Genius
afflicted with hypacusia. Music, time of redemption, of utopia.
No one's ready to accept it.
No one knows how to conjoin with Beethoven.
Sounds, marks, and notes, high in number, always minor,
will conduct to a trick.
The absurdity is that one has consciousness of his emptiness
and the other one, annihilated, doesn't have an identity.
But if a ticket, one-way, to Amsterdam,
is found in the inside pocket of his ja-
cket, Gentlemen, have no doubt, I am that man.

Ad immagine dell'infinito

« La clessidra dell'esistenza viene sempre di nuovo
capovolta e tu con essa . . . »
—Friedrich Nietzsche, *La gaia scienza*

La gravità zelante di un valletto, in ombra,
sul cono più alto, stagnante, ad ogni soprassalto.
Estraniato. Nella bonaccia. Sul palcoscenico di vetro
si illude di mandare fuori tempo il congegno.
Tempo rubato. Dilazionato.
All'improvviso si sente mancare la terra sotto i piedi,
mentre si avvicina alla gola che apre al sottomondo segreto,
non può tornare indietro, sospinto, a capofitto declina
in tante traiettorie frenetiche, sul fondo,
stilla come sangue da una stretta ferita,
scontroso, perché sa che non potrà abitare
le stesse posizioni ogni volta che la clessidra
sarà sovvertita.
Ma c'è qualcosa che lo umanizza,
che oltrepassa e trascende il tempo.
Perduto?
Ritrovato?
O un irreversibile salto verso il nulla?
E rovesciato, nell'aria, inizia un nuovo ciclo
verso un tempo nuovo di cui è arduo carpire l'intensità
di ciò che passa, o anche la tenuità,
difficile esibire immagini coerenti della nostra presenza,
scoprire un'effettiva, reale, misura interiore,
per comporre tutti questi frammenti(di sabbia)
in pensieri dicibili.
Dicci pure, Louis Borges: fu realmente di miele
l'ultima goccia attingibile della tua clessidra?

Towards the infinite

> "The eternal hourglass of existence is turned upside down
> again and again, and you with it . . ."
> —Friedrich Nietzsche, *The Gay Science*

The zealous gravity of a valet, in shadow,
on the upper cone stagnant, with every start.
Estranged. In the lull.   On the glass stage
he lives the illusion that the device keeps time out.
Stolen time. Delayed.
Suddenly you feel the absence of ground under your feet,
as it approaches its throat, opening to the secret underworld,
there's no going back, a push, headlong decline
in so many frenetic trajectories, forming around the bottom,
drips like blood from a narrow wound,
surly, because each time the hourglass is upended
it knows it will not be able to inhabit
the same positions.
But there is something that humanizes it,
something overstepping and transcending time.
Lost?
Found?
Or an irreversible leap towards nothing?
And overturned, in the air, a new cycle begins
towards a new time, the intensity, or the tenuity,
of which, and figuring out what happens next, is grueling,
it's difficult exhibiting images coherent to our presence,
discovering an actual, real, interior, measurement,
for composing all of these (sand)fragments
in speakable thoughts.
Oh tell us, really, Louis Borges: was the last drop that could be
tapped from your hourglass truly honey?

La porta girevole

A R. Musil

Ruota la porta girevole in senso antiorario
la successione di vuoto crea la distanza
tra chi precede e chi segue
immagini in sovrapposizione atti rallentati attese
quale diabolico diletto l'espressione cortese del poeta
istituzionalizzato in quella permanenza ineluttabile
medita di smantellare la porta /o l'attesa?/
trasfigurandola in metafora qualcosa che accoglie
respinge cattura e libera sgomenta in quella luce
mistica potrebbe imitare l'uccello leggendario
piumaggio caldo arancione testa d'uomo coda di pavone
vedendosi riflesso nella lastra di vetro contemplandosi
da il la ad un canto tristissimo e . . .   muore
il Simurg/o il poeta?/
dominio del tempo scenico l'indugio in un gioco di quinte
d'angolo sul fondalino l'inattesa svolta inelegante ordinario
l'uomo avanti a se non c'è davvero nessun altro dentro il tempio
pagano perde coscienza il vate declama l'altro
neppure alza lo sguardo peggio per lui esclama
in questo frammento /di tempo/è il momento più alto
la mia poesia tragedia della porta girevole la testa calva
perdura a declamare con Artaud:
Ahimè un poeta non può rinchiudersi vigliaccamente
in un luogo da cui non uscirà più
il tempo si dilata sull'orlo dell'istante si riapre la porta
  continua a ruotare
L'uomo senza qualità un avventore inquietante.

The Revolving Door

To R. Musil

The revolving door turns counterclockwise
the resulting emptiness creates distance
between whoever goes first and whoever follows
images superimposed   slowed-down   actions expected
which diabolic delight the lovely expression
of the poet institutionalized in that ineluctable permanence
meditates on dismantling the door /or the wait?/
transfiguring it into metaphor something that embraces
repels captures and liberates dismays in that mystical
light it might imitate the mythical bird
hot orange plumage man's head peacock's tail
seeing itself reflected in the sheet of glass contemplating itself
begins a very sad song and . . . does the Simurgh
die/or the poet?/
dominion of the scenic time the delay in a game of scenery
of the angle on the little backdrop the unforeseen turning point
inelegant ordinary the man in front of himself there's really
no one else inside the pagan temple
he loses consciousness il vate declaims the other
not even lifting his gaze his loss he exclaims
in this fragment /of time/this is the most elevated moment
my tragedy poetry of the revolving door shaved head
persists in declaiming   with Artaud:
Alas a poet cannot withdraw into himself cowardly
into a place from which he will never emerge
time expands on the edge of the instant one   reopens the door
 it continues to turn
The man without quality a distressing customer.

Alétheia Alétheia

E' l'inganno una visione utopica del mondo?

Chissà quanti tipi di inganno esistono nella vita . . .

Ebbene, la storia parla di un uomo

che ha saputo ingannarsi

banali inganni s'intende
menzogne della mente
autoinganni per controbilanciare

la consapevolezza

l'attendibilità
una visione del mondo
che ha
una sua presa
sulla realtà

E così per tutto il tempo il movimento
è stato assicurato
dalla mutazione
di sé stesso.
Nessuna stagnazione
senso di vertigine
trascuratezza
ordinarietà

Alétheia Alétheia

Is deceit a utopic vision of the world?

Who knows how many types of deceits exist in life . . .

Well, then, the story tells of a man

who knew how to deceive himself

commonplace deceits understand
untruths of the mind
self-deceptions to counterbalance

consciousness

credence
a vision of the world
that has
its own hold
on reality

And in this way the whole time
movement
the changing of himself
was guaranteed.
No stagnation
sense of vertigo
carelessness
mediocrity

Che senso ha negarlo?
La storia non si può abbellire

ora che certi segni

han detto
che non potrà più
ingannarsi
che non potrà più
finanziare idee tra loro inconciliabili
han detto che presto
 molto presto
non avrà più la possibilità

di scrivere

 di parlare

di vedere

che non avrà più la possibilità

 di vivere.

 Alétheia, Alétheia . . .

Why deny it?
History cannot be made pretty

now that certain signs

have said
he won't be able to deceive himself
any longer
he won't be able to finance incompatible ideas among the
      irreconcilable ones
any longer
they've said that soon
  very soon
he won't have the possibility anymore

of writing

  of speaking

of seeing

that he won't have the possibility anymore

  of living.

  Alétheia, Alétheia . . .

I fantasmi della mente

Bellezza origine e ultimità del cosmo in occhi verdi
sognanti il nastro della felicità tra i capelli
nessuna asperità nessun affanno interiore
Volgere via lo sguardo chiamarlo altrove
lei non vivrebbe di là dalla cornice lungo dirupi
sentieri non tracciati in cerca del rimosso
l'impensato il mancante le cose che si lasciano
intuire quelle invisibili segrete

A volte si riesce a vedere prati fioriti ovunque
svelare il turbamento le cose che non si fanno riconoscere
e che non ti riconoscono
Altre volte la realtà si avvicina si rivela troppo in fretta
il talento la amplifica così il pensare fuori dagli schemi
le idee oltre misura estranee alla tradizione
esuberanti inusuali fermenti eccessivi fulminei
i fantasmi della mente tendono un' imboscata

Dici di stare in guardia? Da cosa? Dall'euforia? dall'assillo?
La depressione La mania? Le allucinazioni Le ossessioni?
  La fobia? Le torbide passioni ? L'isteria? L'ansia di draghi rossi
e salamandre che gettano fuoco su di te?

A volte capita di udire da lontano una musica
che copre l' inquietudine qualcuno ha l'impressione
che siano gli stessi soggetti a seminare paure
e a comporre musica

Ghosts of the Mind

Original beauty and ultimiteness of the cosmos in dreamy
green eyes the ribbon of happiness in hair
no bitterness whatsoever no internal grief
Directing the gaze away calling it elsewhere
she would not live outside the frame along cliffs
unmarked paths in search of reliving
the unforeseen the lacking the things left
for intuiting those invisible secrets

Sometimes we do get to see fields blooming wherever
restlessness reveals things they do not let us recognize
and that do not recognize you
Other times reality draws close revealing too much too quickly
its gift amplifying it so that thought outside the frameworks
the ideas alien to tradition beyond measure
exuberant uncanny agitated excessive lightning-quick
the ghosts of the mind tend to move towards an ambush

Should you tell yourself to be on guard? From what? From
      euphoria?
from worry? Depression? Mania? Hallucination?
Obsessions? Phobia? Turbulent passions? Hysteria? Anxiety
about red dragons and salamanders shooting fire   on you?

Sometimes it does happen   hearing from far off a music
that covers agitation someone has the impression
it is the same subjects seeding fear
and composing music

E' successo a Robert Schumann rinchiuso in un istituto mentale
di Bonn le partiture deliziose le note che ci ha affidato e le paure
dell'acqua degli spazi aperti delle altitudini
paura di essere avvelenato diventare un altro e avvertiva il
    suono
  continuo *"di lontani ottoni che diventava coro di angeli*
che cantavano una melodia che lui inutilmente cercava di
    trascrivere"
E non aveva ricevuto il bacio da Anne Sexton *i nervi sono accesi e*
il compositore è entrato nel fuoco
dove fa il nido la salamandra a corto di veleno e il pieno
il drago rosso improvvido custode del vello d'oro.

La tua idea fissa è che quelle pennellate evidenti
fioriture nel dipinto e quel volto sublime ti volteggino intorno
offrendoti le più sorprendenti rivelazioni e tutto con una musica
idilliaca di un pianoforte /che per la gente ordinaria
può tacere tutta la vita/ magari quella musica è un *Improvviso*
in do maggiore di Schumann

La fanciulla con il nastro turchese tra i capelli
sorride

It did happen to   Robert Schumann shut up in a mental
        institution
in Bonn the gorgeous score the notes to which he
entrusted fears of water and open spaces heights
fear of being poisoned of becoming someone else and he
        perceived continuous sound "*of faroff*
brass that became a chorus of angels singing
a melody he tried in vain to transcribe"
And he had not received the kiss from Anne Sexton *the nerves*
        are turned on and the composer has stepped into the fire.
where in lieu of poison the salamander makes nest and fullness
the red the improvident dragon guards the golden fleece

Your fixed idea is only the ones in painted brush strokes obvious
flowering in the picture and that sublime face and they spin inside
        you offering you the most surprising revelations and all
with an idyllic music of a piano /that can silence ordinary people
their whole lives/ maybe that music is an *Improvisation*
in C major by Schumann.

The girl with the turquoise ribbon in her hair
smiles

Palio di Siena

Zampe smagrite . . .
  vigorose   unite
di rincorsa tra i canapi
la mossa
il tripudio del sole
sulle mura ad arginare
la folla
e il suo delirio

L'irrequieto scudiscio
su la schiena del barbero
che assottiglia lo sguardo
verso il drappo
che designa
il corsiero invincibile

Palio of Siena

Legs that have shed lots of weight . . .
  vigorous   united
in the race amidst the ropes.
la mossa,
the sun sparkling
on the city walls to contain
the mob
and its delirium

The restless whip
against the back of the barbary
which thins the gaze
in the direction of the banner
designating
the invincible race-horse

L'Universo e gli anelli

Atomi di spazio, cammini chiusi, la perfezione sferica di anelli
che intessono, con altri, ariose reti di relazioni per dar vita
allo spazio tempo, con la sua curvatura inverosimile, finché
una nana bianca, stella degenere, evanescente, volle dare
la prova inconfutabile che la superficie dell'universo è curva,
conseguenza della massa dei corpi celesti contenuti.
Fune che si flette sotto il peso del funambolo. Il cosmo è tutto
un fremito, un gran vibrare. La bellezza di suoni e colori,
plurime risonanze, tonali ambiguità. Aperto è il suono che
dal silenzio perviene. Il silenzio appartiene al suono. L'insieme
dei possibili suoni, neutro bigio, è una forma di silenzio.
    Grigio
bianco, che il candore difende, è il connubio di tutti i colori.
Colore è cadenza di luce. Dall'esigua frequenza sorge il rosso,
al viola la preminenza. L'alta ciclicità giova all'energia.
Il suono chiama, il colore, sorretto da luce ed ombre, risponde,
domina ben oltre il sistema solare, imperversa il rosso
    di Antares,
gigante, e di Betelgeuse, disperatamente in fase terminale.
Lo sfolgorante bianco di Sirio e di Vega, più fulgente del Sole,
in un Universo dove primeggia il nero- grigio dello spazio
    vuoto
fra galassia e galassia. Dai padiglioni del mondo ascoltava
Pitagora, il lungimirante, quel concerto di colori e suoni,
con i suoi numerici rapporti, archetipi della forma, onde
che fuggono lungo corde tese vibranti, come quelle di
    un violino.

The Universe and the Rings

Atoms of space, closed paths, the spheric perfection of rings
interweaving, with others, airy nets of relationships giving life
to spacetime, with its unbelievable curvature, until
a white dwarf, degenerate star, evanescent, meant
the surface of the universe is curved, incontrovertible proof,
consequence of the mass of celestial bodies contents.
Rope that bends under the weight of the rope walker. The cosmos
is one big trembling, a great vibrating. The beauty of sounds
        and colors,
multiple resonances, tonal ambiguity. Sound arriving
from silence is open. Silence belongs to sound. The totality
of possible sounds, neutral ash-gray, is a form of silence. White
gray, which candor defends, is the union of all of the colors.
Color is the cadence of light. From the low frequency red
        emerges
to violet's preeminence. The great cyclicity is an advantage to
        energy.
Sound calls, color, sustained by light and shadow, responds,
dominating far beyond the solar system, the red of giant Antares
and of Betelgeuse, desperately in terminal phase, rages.
The dazzling white of Sirius and Vega, more radiant than the Sun,
in a Universe where the black-gray of space void between galaxy
and galaxy stands out. From the pavilions of the world, forward-
looking Pythagoras was listening to that concert of colors and
        sounds,
with their numerical correspondences, archtypes of the form,
        waves
running away along stretched vibrating cords, like the ones on a
        violin.

Quale uomo ha avuto altrettanta influenza nel campo del
   pensiero?
Dante, il divino, sicuramente ha percepito il suono delle sfere,
riconosciuto come atto della mente: *l'armonia che temperi e
   discerni.*

Sulle spalle dei giganti è salito Newton con il suo corteo di colori
e di luce per vedere più avanti, e raccontare il mondo, dove dal
   nulla
affiorano particelle, scompaiono con le loro stranezze,
   irraggiungibili,
nemmeno fossero raggi di astri sperduti nel loro moto. L'azzurro
profondo è un vuoto che molto ha da elargire. Si animano
   processi,
strutture, turbamenti per le inedite forme, la realtà concreta
si manifesta da questa scaturigine. Sfocata è la visione di appannati
mondi, lontani. L'intenzione non è di annullare la distanza,
   piegarsi
al disordine, alla casualità, ma riconoscerle. Nel contempo nuovi
varchi si schiudono verso l'invisibile, ai confini dei luoghi
   dell'assenza.
E sempre ci sorprende ogni concezione inquietante dell'Universo.
Ma che cosa guida la realtà? Domandare! Le domande ci abitano
misteriosamente. Domandare! Domandare sempre, e di nuovo.
Avrebbe voluto, Pound, che le onde fredde della sua mente
fluttuassero, che il mondo si inaridisse come una foglia morta,
e fosse spazzato via per ritrovare, sola, quella donna.
Ma qui, oltre all'intelletto, a fluttuare sono campi quantistici,
lo spazio interstellare. E' questo dimenarsi di quanti che elegge
particelle onde quark/i veri mattoni del mondo/. Le loro danze,
i loro incontri, non avranno lo stesso fascino di Francesca,
ma sono anch'esse una mousikè, cornice di bellezza, di assoluta
   verità.
Poco altro inaridisce oltre alla foglia morta, se non l'uomo

What other man had such influence in the field of thought?
Dante, the divine, surely had perceived the sound of the spheres,
recognized as an act of the mind: *l'armonia che temperi e discerni.*

Newton climbed onto the shoulders of giants with his
        progression of colors
and light for seeing farther, relating the world, where particles
        emerge
from nothing, and fade away, out of reach, with their strangeness,
even as rays of stars lost within their motion. Deep blue is a void
with much to lavish. Processes, structures, emotions over
new forms come to life, concrete reality shows itself
from this source. The vision of these hazy, distant worlds
is out of focus. The intention is not to nullify distance, caving
in to disorder, to chance, but to recognize them. At the same
        time new
crossings open up towards the invisible at the limits of places of
        absence.
And every unsettling concept about the Universe always
        surprises us.
What is it that's guiding reality? Ask! Questions mysteriously
live with us. Ask! Ask always, and again.
He, Pound, would have wanted the cold waves of his mind to
        fluctuate
so the world would wither like a dead leaf
and be swept away in order to find that woman, alone.
But here, beyond the intellect, are quantum fields, fluctuating,
interstellar space. It's this thrashing around of quanta electing
quark waves particles/the real brick and mortar of the
        world/. Their dances,
their encounters, will not hold the same fascination as Francesca,
but even these are a mousikè, a framework of beauty, of absolute
        truth.
Little besides man inside the labyrinth of existence

dentro al labirinto dell'esistenza, la fedeltà disperata al pianeta.
Smarrite, alla fine, le proprie ceneri come polveri cosmiche
minute, grigio scure. Pure espressioni di esigenza interiore le tele
di Kandinskij incendiano i sensi oltrepassando i limiti, le singole
percezioni. Il pensiero si addentra nell'Universo stellare per
    leggervi
l'animazione che ci sfugge, per condividerne l'irrefrenabile
    pulsare.

with his desperate loyalty to the planet, withers more than the
    dead leaf.
Lost, in the end, his own ashes like minute, dark gray
cosmic dust. Pure expressions of interior necessity, the canvases
of Kandinsky set the senses on fire, went beyond the limits, single
perceptions. Thought penetrates into the stellar Universe to read
the animation inside it that escapes us, in order to share in the
    irrepressible pulsar.

Ritratto del Padre

Sul pianeta Mercurio c'è un cratere
quello di Dürer e negli Uffizi
olio su tavola il ritratto del padre
a mezzo busto girato di tre quarti
verso sinistra sfondo buio
colbacco di pelliccia una maglietta scura
e una casacca viola larghi segni sul viso
la quieta coscienza
ora provi tenerezza nel guardare la figura
ti fa sentire più sicuro
ora sai quanto è difficile parlarne
qui per fortuna non ti chiedono parole
nemmeno di raccontare te stesso
così non hai bisogno di traslare storie
di un padre che sentivi come un salvacondotto
e di un figlio sedotto dalla ribellione
contrapporsi scindersi tenersi fuori separati distinti
nessuno slancio da parte sua a svelare l'anima
forse se stesso rivedeva nel figlio
era un suo diritto nessun si sentirà di biasimarlo
una volta i padri erano fatti così
apparteneva il sentimento al pudore
ritenevano giusto esercitare la patria potestas
nessuna mancanza di generosità
adesso rimpiangi le tensioni di allora
vorresti che tornasse la sua mano il suo sguardo volgesse
su di te perché ora sai obbedire e tutto ti appare

Portrait of the Father

On the planet Mercury there is a crater
Dürer's and in the Uffizi
the portrait of the father, oil on panel
half-length turned in three-quarter view
towards the left dark background
fur hat of pelts dark undergarment,
and a violet tunic large marks on his face
quiet conscience
now you experience tenderness in looking at the figure
it gives you feelings of security
now you know how difficult it is to talk about it
here luckily they don't ask you for words
not even to talk about yourself
so you don't have to transfer
a father's stories   having heard them like a safe-conduct
and those of a son seduced by the rebellion
counterposing differentiating keeping a distance separated distinct
not one impulse coming from him to reveal the soul
maybe he saw himself again in the son
it was one of his rights no one will criticize him
fathers were made that way at one time
he was part of the emotion, reserve
they held it to be true and just to exercise the patria potestas
no lack whatsoever of generosity
now you're lamenting the bygone tensions
you would like his hand to return his gaze to turn back
over you because now you understand obeying and everything
    seems

rispettabile ma in quel tempo bramavi
quanto c'era di aspro di ribelle
non lo amavi abbastanza
Lui suonava il clarino e tu agognavi il pianoforte
l'Andante per corno e piano concepito da Richard Strauss
non sapevi a vent'anni che era un dono
del giovane compositore al proprio genitore
eppure era stato lui a guidarti
sui primi gradini delle scale dei suoni
nei suoi momenti preziosi
sospesi sopra il mondo attraversato
dalla tua impazienza

Fatica il figlio ad entrare nel tempo
da quando il padre non c'è più
e non c'è nulla che possa bilanciare
il tempo profano avaro di questa vita

respectable but at that time you craved
how much there was of the harshness of the rebel
you did not love him enough
He played the clarinet and you aspired to the piano
Andante for horn and piano conceived by Richard Strauss
at twenty you didn't know it was a gift
of the young composer to his own parent
it was him in fact guiding you
on the first steps of sounds
in the invaluable   moments
suspended above the world crossing over
your impatience

The son struggles entering into time
once the father is no more
and there's nothing that can balance
the profane mean time of this life

Identità

Il presente: la sola dimensione.
E ha perso il nome, l'essenza, causa sui
e per l'azione di famulus miserandi fautori dell'espansione,
corruttori d'identità.
Fletto la passività, sfato la connessione, frantumo gli
    argini,
l'indolenza che assume valenza metafisica.
A lungo fu il grigio degli sguardi
ora un piccolo astro rosso lucente
lumeggia nella mente come esigenza di un luogo limpido,
nuovo d'aria e di luce.
(contro-voce)
Senza paesaggio che lo distingua, con troppi punti
di approdo, troppi crocevia da oltrepassare.
Una trappola claustrofobica.
La fiera globale non è poi così male, spinge lo sviluppo,
riduce la povertà, vale l'adagio del sempre ci sarà chi
    affligge
e qualcun altro che sarà oppresso,
e poi . . . esiste la libertà intera?
In mare o terra, scortato dal miraggio seducente,
fra l'istante di un crollo nell'abisso e il ritorno alla vita,
lascia dall'altro lato il servaggio, l'inedito è di fronte,
l'impazienza di scoprire la propria identità
l'idea di sé difforme dagli altri, e di sé attraverso il tempo.

Identity

The present: the only dimension.
And it's lost name, essence, cause
on the and because of the action of famulus pitiful upholders of
    expansion,
corruptors of identity.
I bend the resignation, unmask the connection, make
    embankments crumble,
the indolence metaphysical value assumes.
For a long time there was the gray of the gazing
now a small red shining star
highlights inside the mind like necessity for a clear place,
with new air and with new light.
(counter-voice)
Without the landscape that distinguishes it, with its too many
    landing
points, too many intersections for crossing over into.
A claustrophonic trap.
The global fair isn't so bad then, it does push for development,
it does reduce poverty, it's true always going slowly, there will
    always be those
who afflict and another who will be oppressed,
and also . . . does liberty, whole, exist ?
Escorted by the seductive mirage, by land or sea,
between the instant of collapse into the abyss and the return to
    life,
serfdom departs from one shore, what's unknown lies ahead,
the impatience to discover one's own identity,
the idea of oneself dissimilar from the others, and of oneself
    across time.

Sincronico e diacronico, — direbbe Saussure.

Co-abitare l'isola, antica come il mito.

Perché nessuno la nomina?

Perché gli echi sono inaudibili?

In quell'arcaica natura in cui si raccolgono le ombre,

mani come rami stringono altre mani, arbusti sempreverdi,

compatti, ricadenti sulla terra vermiglia, s' incontrano

fra spigliate fioriture di intenso color lilla, rosse bacche fragranti.

Una sorta di Origine.

E c'è chi, affrancato, scuote le catene, festosamente,

chi sente come un'epifania la contorsione di quel corpo

accorso dietro una promessa che l'animale-uomo

è legittimato a fare: das versprechen darf.

Certi danzano, ridono, altri parlano un lessico ermetico,
      inconsueto.

E' forse necessario un nuovo linguaggio? Un idioma segreto?

Co-abito l'inquietudine, il dubbio che tradisce, scruto in faccia
      l'incertezza,

per capirne il senso.

La mancata dialettica non lascia individuare inediti scenari,
      antidoti

alla coazione a ripetere, /vero elemento demoniaco/, la
      dimensione

dell'agire, saggiare la vertigine della libertà che ad ognuno dovrà
      rivelarsi.

Majakovskij tuonava: /Noi la dialettica non l'imparammo da
      Hegel /

quando sotto i proiettili /dinnanzi a noi fuggivano i borghesi,/

Qui, alcuni fuggono, ripiegano, tenendo in petto, semplicemente,

il senso di vertigine, il mancato riscatto.

Arretrano. Volgono i passi, si consegnano alla prassi.

E i crolli? Le macerie ammassate sulla via?

Eretto intorno all'isola, o forse nella mente, l'archivolto azzurro-
      cielo

Synchronic and diachronic,—Saussure would say.
Co-habiting the island, ancient as the myth.
Why did no one name it?
Why are the echoes inaudible?
In that archaic nature where the shadows are concentrated,
hands like branches are grasping other hands, compact evergreen
shrubs hanging over the vermillion ground, meeting among
        fluent
blossoms intensely colored lilac and pink fragrant berries.
A destiny of Origin.
And there are those who have liberated themselves, who break
        the chains
joyfully, who feel the contortion of that body like an epiphany
realizing that behind a promise the man-animal
is legitmized making: das versprechen darf.
Some dance, laugh, others speak a rare hermetic lexicon.
Is perhaps a new language necessary? A secret idiom?
I co-habitate with apprehension, the doubt it's betraying,
I study the face of uncertainty to make sense of it.
The dialectics lacking don't permit the pinpointing of unknown
scenarios, antidotes to repetition's coaction, /true demonic
        element/,
dimension of effect, testing liberty's confusion which will have to
        reveal itself to everyone.
Majakovsky thundered: We did not learn dialectics from Hegel /
        when we were faced / under fire the bourgeois fled, /
Here, some flee, retreat, simply keeping the sense of confusion
close to the chest, no release.
They withdraw. They direct their steps, consign themselves to
        routine.
And the collapses? The ruins heaped on the road?
The blue-sky archivolt, erect around the island, or maybe in the
        mind,

sorregge l'utopia perché il mondo non sia più come un non so
    che di apparente.
L'esperienza gradualmente si invera.
In evidenza l'effettiva Identità, la memoria,
stili di vita relegati ai margini, in penombra le paure, le
    perplessità.
Per gioia ogni voce diventerà riconoscibile.
Nessuno incererà "de' compagni /senza dimora/ le orecchie",
  per godere la bellezza del canto delle sirene,
più deliziose che mai.
Nella congiuntura le incantatrici ritroveranno,
definitivamente, la loro dionisiaca voce.

supports utopia so that the world is no longer something illusory
and undefined.
Experience gradually proves true.
Demonstrating real Identity, memory,
lifestyles relegated to the margins, fears, perplexity, in semi-
darkness.
Each voice will become recognizable out of joy.
No one will put wax into "the ears/of companions/with no
home,"
in order to enjoy the beauty of the sirens' song
more delicious than ever.
At the conjuncture the enchantresses once again, definitely,
will find their dionysian voice.

Grattacielo

Scale di suono e silenzio
brillano di luci oscure
mosse verso il cielo
o verso i gradini in declivio

Quanti ne ammireranno le altezze
Quanti apprezzano le profondità

La vita ha desiderio di sommità
di calde parole
la gravità è un folletto che le riconduce indietro
la caduta le raffredda

O la vetta o il baratro il dubbio resta
ma non restare naso all'insù per tutto il tempo
se non per ammirare la volta stellata
E non fissare lo sguardo nella forra
Potrebbe il serpente prima o poi
aggrovigliarti la gola
Se l'elevazione produce *vertigine*
la discesa propizia la depressione
A chi si trova sul fondo
il Lettore Supremo sul tetto
pare troppo distante
poi si avvicina e scopre
che non è così

Skyscraper

Stairs of sound and silence
sparkle with dim indistinct lights
movements towards the sky
or towards steps on a downward slope

How many will admire the heights of it
How many appreciate the depths

Life longs for the summit
for hot words
gravity's a sprite bringing them back
the fall cools them

Whether it's the peak or the abyss
doubt remains but not with nose in the air
for all time unless it's for admiring the starry vault.
And not for staring into the chasm
It might be sooner or later the serpent
is wrapped round your throat
If heights produce *vertigo*
the decline propitiates depression.
For whomever finds himself at the bottom
the Reader Supreme on the roof
seems too distant
then he draws closer and discovers
not so

In quale piano deve dimorare il poeta?
La mente dimora fuori dal grattacielo
sei solo tu Eraclito ad affermare:
"la via in su ed in giù è unica ed identica"
più coerente pensare che siano
due orientamenti
di una unica insensata direzione

On what level should the poet dwell?
The mind dwells outside the skyscraper
it's only you Heraclitus affirming:
"the path up and down are one and the same"
more coherent thinking there are
two orientations
of a single insensate direction

Dioniso

Nel suo mantello di pantera, bizzarro
come la madre Semele, figlia di mortali,
apre il corteggio di ninfe senza veli,
satiri dalle zampe caprine, fra le vigne,
sopra le colline, azzurrate di rame.
Dioniso creatore della vite, e del vino,
signore del risveglio e dell'istinto
accoglie la baccante più bella, Arianna
per celebrare un rito fatto di tralci
e grappoli maturi al sole della vita.
Fremono cesoie diamantate nel gesto
generoso, audace, moriranno d'amore
i chicchi, e al primo soffio di vento
salirà l'odore inebriante dai tini.
Flauti, timpani, lyre ad animare
danze e canzoni, a dischiudere i sensi
alla felicità. Mutano in incanti
assillanti pensieri, ogni bieco tormento.
Gli uomini di senno gettano le spade,
raccolgono le note più alte, degustano,
in ogni suo piacere, il vino, rosso
talismano che li rende saggi, immortali,
scoprono arcani misteri, virtù rare,
lieti di scorgere nel fondo del bicchiere
le nitide impronte della   divinità.

Dionysus

In his panther mantle, bizarre
as his mother Semele daughter of mortals,
he leads the procession of unveiled nymphs
and satyrs with goat hooves through the vineyards
to hilltops turned coppery blue.
Creator of grapevines, and wine, master
of arousal and instinct, Dionysus welcomed
Ariadne, the most beautiful bacchante,
to celebrate a ritual made with vine shoots
and clusters of grapes ripened under a sun in full life.
Diamond-shaped shears tremble at the lavishingly
bold gesture, grapes will die out of love
and the inebriating scent will rise up
out of the vats with the first breath of wind.
Flutes, timpani, lyres for enlivening dances
and songs and for opening up the senses
to bliss. Nagging thoughts and every dark
agony transform under a spell.
Sensible men throw aside their swords,
harvesting the highest notes, imbibing
in every pleasure, wine, the red
talisman making them wisemen, immortals,
they discover arcane mysteries, rare virtues,
content glimpsing at the bottom of the glass
the clear tracks of the   divinity.

Nella terra e nella musica

A Claudio Ferrarini, flautista

Tre poemi dai contorni sfuggenti
di Stéphane Mallarmé
le riveste il geniale Claude Debussy
di sonorità sfumate
colore effetti di sospensione armonie
il sottile ticchettio dell'istinto
l'enigmatico pulsare della Natura

Apertura uomo terra   pura
La mente se ne va agli anni
del Prix de Rome a L'enfant prodige

Il giovane Debussy
non poteva credere ai propri occhi:
piegato in avanti nessun altra esecuzione
lo avrebbe fatto curvare così tanto
cappello a larghe tese e stivali
la zappa ben stretta
nessuno avrebbe potuto trattenerla più salda
e era Giuseppe Verdi.
Scuoteva lento il capo
il maestro lo scrutava senza parlare
e presto riprese a inabissare lo sguardo
fra corrugate zolle minute pietre
convesse lisce a un'incredibile profondità

In earth and music

To Claudio Ferrarini, flutist

Three poems with elusive outlines
by Stéphane Mallarmé
the brilliant Claude Debussy
tried them on again with softened richness
colors accomplished by suspension harmony
faint ticking of instinct
enigmatic pulsating of Nature

Opening man   pure   earth
The mind goes the way of the years
the Prix de Rome to L'Enfant Prodige

The young Debussy
could not believe his own eyes:
bent over in front of him   no other execution
would have made him curve as much
soft-brimmed hat drooping and boots
the hoe straight
no one else could have carried himself as firmly
and it was   Giuseppe Verdi.
He shook his head slowly
the maestro   examined him without speaking
and his gaze shifted it sank
among corrugated clods   minute
stones   into an incredible convex smooth depth

fin sotto la radice nei solchi sotterranei del mito
a snidare il segreto del mondo
l'origine divina delle cose
Fino a quel silenzio
E qui è
          l'Inizio
  E qui è la
                FINE.

all the way down to the root in the subterranean furrows of myth
to untangle the secret of the world
the divine origin of things
As far as that silence
And here is
        the Beginning
And here is
           the End.

Notes

DIOMEDES

The name of the Diomede Islands, located in the Bering Strait, is derived from Diomedes, one of the great Greek heroes of the Trojan War. Diomedes, a central figure in Homer's *Iliad*, is the epitome of heroic values, including excellence in battle, bravery, self-restraint, leadership, and the love of justice and friendship. A figure associated with the spreading of Greek civilization and culture, Diomedes is central to many legends, including one in which he threw large stones into the Adriatic Sea and they emerged as islands.

ABOVE THE SENSE OF THE VOID

Ténéré. A desert region in the south central Sahara, stretching from northeastern Niger into western Chad. The word is derived from the Tuareg word for *desert*; in Berber it is called, *Tiniri*, meaning *desert* or *wilderness*.

Le Rondini / Swallows. The epigraph is from "Pasqua 1952," by Leonardo Sinisgalli.

Sollers tempus / Sollers tempus. Skillful time. See William Shakespeare, Sonnet 126. "She keeps thee to this purpose, that her skill"

Da lontano, molto da lontano . . . / From a distance, a great distance . . . l. 11. the seventh-compartment. The seventh car of a train is a symbol death, derived from The Book of Joshua. "In the seventh compartment dwell those who died from illnesses caused through the sins of Israel."

IF THE MOON WERE A KITE

In Greek mythology, the sculptor Pygmalion of Cyprus fell in love with a beautiful statue of ivory. After making offerings to the altar of Aphrodite, the statue came to life. Galatea is the woman born out of the statue.

NOTEBOOKS FROM THE USSERO

Avatar / Avatar. l. 10. omnes gradus. all levels.

La porta girevole / The Revolving Door. l. 18. il vate. *Poeta vate* is a title derived from ancient Rome and conferred to poets who attempt to interpret and guide public sentiment of a given age. Gabriele D'Annunzio, for example, was referred to as *il Vate*.

Alétheia Alétheia. Alétheia. From the Greek, λήθεια. The state or action of opening. The state or action of unveiling. Truth as defined by what is unconcealed and not being hidden.

L'Universo e gli anelli (The Universe and the Rings). l. 26. "*l'armonia che temperi e discerni.*" (with Harmony which tempers and discerns) from Dante Alighieri, the *Paradiso* of the *Divina Comedia*, Canto I, 79. Translated as "With strains which Thou doest tune and modulate," by Dorothy Sayers in the Penguin 2004 edition. The passage is translated by Clive James as follows: "Now your eternal wheel— / Constructed and set spinning by desire— / Held me intent by what it made me feel, / Its harmony. Your voices form a choir / In tune, and spread among the spheres . . ." 88–92. W.W. Norton & Co. 2013 edition.

Palio di Siena (Palio of Siena) ll. 3–4. di rincorsa tra i canapi / la mossa (in the race amidst the ropes. / the drop,) The *canape* is the rope dropped to signal the beginning of the Palio. The moment when the *canape* is dropped to signal the start of the race is called *la mossa*, a noun derived from the verb *muovere* (to move).

Berbero. ll. 2.2. su la schiena del berbero (against the back of the Barbero). The horses assigned to race from each contrada were originally Barbary horses from North Africa. Most of the horses competing in the Palio of Siena today are Sardinian Anglo-Arab.

"Il grattacielo" (Skyscraper). "Il grattacielo," carries references to the prose piece, "Il grattacielo," by philosopher and social scientiest Max Horkheimer (1895–1973), more for its imagery of verticality and stratification than for its critique of modern civlzatation, according to de Robertis. Horkheimer was a leader of the Frankfurt School of critical thinking. Horkheimer's "Il grattacielo" was published as *Crepuscolo: Appunti presi in Germania, 1926–1931*, in a translation by Giorgio Backhaus, (Einaudi, 1977).

Bibliography

POETRY

Diomedee, Edizioni Joker, Novi Ligure, Alessandria, 2008.

Sovra il Senso del Vuoto, Novastampa Ponsacco, Pisa. 2009.

Se La Luna fosse un Aquilone, Editore Limina Mentis, Villasanta (MB), 2012.

I Quaderni dell'Ussero, puntoacapo Editrice Novi Ligure, Alessandria, 2013.

Parti del discorso (poetico), Marco del Bucchia Editore, Massarosa (Lucca), 2014.

NOVELS

L'Epigono di Magellano, Edizioni Akkuaria, 2012.

Il tempo dorme con noi, Primo Premio Internazionale Giovanni Gronchi, 1999.

Acknowledgments

Grateful acknowledgment is made to editor and publisher Marco del Bucchia for the following poems, published in *Parti del discorso (poetico)* (2014) by Marco del Bucchia Editore: La Terra Promessa, La Chiave, Come Furfanti, Il Paese, E guardi il mare, Formiche, Quasi mai, Isole, Gli incomodi pensieri, Girasoli, A capo chino, Lola, Doppelgänger, Ho quasi consumato, Arno, Ruotare attorno ad una stella, La volta che, Tutto ci avvolge in un unico sguardo, Galileo. Grateful acknowlegment is made to Puntoacapo Edizioni Novi Ligure, which published the poems included from *I Quaderni dell'Ussero* (2013); to Limina Mentis Editore which published the poems included in this volume from *Se La Luna fosse un Aquilone* (2012); to Novastampa Ponsacco, which published the poems included from *Sovra il Senso del Vuoto* (2009), and to Edizioni Joker which published the poems included in this volume from *Diomedee* (2008).

I would like to express my deep gratitude to Ubaldo de Robertis. To Alfredo de Palchi for the invitation to translate these poems. And again to Lisa Cicchetti and to Sarah Candelli.

About the Author

UBALDO de ROBERTIS, born in 1942 in Falerone in the Marche region of Italy, lives in Pisa. His first collection of poetry, *Diomedee*, was published in 2008. *Sovra il Senso del Vuoto* was published in 2009; *Se la Luna fosse un Aquilone* was published in 2012; *I Quaderni dell'Ussero* was published in 2013. He is the author of two novels, *Il tempo dorme con noi* (Voltaire Edizioni), which received the 1999 Giovanni Gronchi award, and *L'Epigono di Magellano* (Edizioni Akkuaria), which was awarded the 2014 Premio Narrativa Fucecchio. His numerous literary prizes include the 2006 il Primo Premio Torre Pendente, and the 2009 Primo Premio Orfici–Omaggio a Dino Campana for *Sovra il Senso del Vuoto*. *Parte del discorso (poetico)* was awarded the 2016 Premio Internazionale di Poesia, Narrativa, e Saggistica. His works have appeared in *Soglie*, *Poiesis*, *La Bottega Letteraria*, *Libere Luci*, and *Homo Eligens*. A researcher in nuclear chemistry, he is a member of the Accademia Nazionale dell'Ussero di Arti, Lettere e Scienze.

About the Translator

ADRIA BERNARDI's translations include *Chronic Hearing: Selected Poems 1977–2012*, poetry of Cristina Annino. She was awarded the 2007 Raiziss/ de Palchi Translation Fellowship to complete *Small Talk*, the poetry of Raffaello Baldini. She is the author of two novels, a collection of short stories, a collection of essays, and an oral history.